GIVING

"A More Excellent Sacrifice"

W0006224

Dr. Cynthia E. Paintsil

Published by

Oasis Publishing Group

Chicago, Illinois.

USA

Website: www.oasispublishinggroup.com

Email: oasispublishinggroup@gmail.com

For copies of the author's book and speaking

engagements contact:

Email: ceepaintsil@gmail.com

ISBN: 979-8-9852806-0-9

**OASIS
PUBLISHING
GROUP**

DEDICATION

I dedicate this book to my amazing mother, Mrs. Rose Ekua Essel, who, by example, taught me how to give. Her faithfulness in paying her tithes, giving offering, honoring the people of God, giving to the poor and needy, and many others, will forever stay with me. As you read through the pages of this book, many of the stories, testimonies, and examples will revolve around her. I hope to pass on this virtue to my children and their children generations to come.

ACKNOWLEDGEMENTS

To God always is all the glory! Thanks to God for giving us the theme "Season of Godliness" in the year 2021. It was in this season that this book was birthed during the teaching/preaching on "Exercising ourselves unto godliness." Many thanks to my husband and Senior Pastor, who has dedicated himself to the work and love of God and His people. As he waited on God to know what His purpose was for the church for the year 2021, he received the theme a "Season of Divine Godliness." Thus, out of this theme as I waited on God to preach was when I received deeper revelations and understanding that "giving, is a spiritual exercise unto godliness". I'd especially like to thank my daughter, Paula, for always typing out all my handwritten manuscripts, (I don't like typing); even though sometimes it's difficult to read, she does a wonderful job with it. My thanks to my family as always for their tremendous support and my Oasis family for the opportunity granted by God to always minister to them as I also get to learn through the process and to all who have been part of my life journey.

PREFACE

I had always believed that I knew and understood the giving of our substance to God as something beyond a natural activity but did not have a deeper understanding of how intensely spiritual it is until God opened my spiritual eyes to comprehend it recently. I began to comprehend this truth from Heb. 11:4 – *"By faith, Abel offered unto God a more excellent sacrifice than Cain, by which he obtained witness that he was righteous, God testifying of his gifts: and by it, he being dead yet speaks."* First, Abel's offering was described as *"a more excellent sacrifice,"* which meant that it was beyond being excellent. Second, by the offering, "he obtained witness that he was righteous" This also means that his offering showed that he had a right standing with God. Third, God himself "testified of his gifts," meaning that God Himself gave evidence to his gifts, and finally, as if all the above was not more than enough, we are told that "by it he being dead yet speaks," which means that even though he (Abel) is dead, through his offering, he continues to speak. Wow! It makes one begin to wonder what manner of offering it was! An offering that continues in perpetuity until this day, even though it was offered since the creation of man on earth more than 6000 years ago? Now, this is what I call an eternal offering! The Holy Spirit took me on a revelational journey, looking into details of all manner of offerings that we give unto God, and interestingly, all of them have deep spiritual significance, including free-will offerings, tithes, alms, and first fruits. Tighten your seatbelts as we explore this journey together.

FOREWORD

We rarely consider the reasons behind such generosity when various forms of charitable activities, whether by individuals or organizations, impress us to the point of applause. We all know or have heard of the millionaires and billionaires who support many worthy projects and the multinationals and non-governmental agencies that make the news with their charitable activities. In most cases, these activities are done from the overabundance of resources or finances and are rarely sacrificial in the sense of providing from a place of pain. When we question the motives behind such giving, we can find a myriad of reasons, including giving back to the community, a sense of obligation to society, a sense of altruism, helping to make the society better, bowing to public pressure, and even as a means of placating the conscience. Rarely, however, is giving connected to biblical principles or articulated in a way that clearly unpacks their various forms, as well as the biblical reasons undergirding them. Understanding these principles and the forms of giving, however, moves the discussion to a level where the reasons are no longer secular but spiritual, a response to a divine summons that emulates God Himself. Assessing giving from this perspective is highly transformative, for it moves us from seeing things from our own narrow perspective to a more transcendental one, something that is higher than us and therefore less selfish. It calls for giving, even when it is painful to do so. If the motivation for giving is linked to the divine, then the reward is assured, not merely from a secular perspective but, more importantly, from the spiritual satisfaction to be derived.

This is what Cynthia Paintsil does in Giving – A More Excellent Sacrifice. In a style that is at once accessible, deep, and thorough, Cynthia Paintsil dispels commonly held beliefs about giving and meticulously demonstrates, with ample scriptural support, that giving is not merely an act of kindness but also a manner of asserting Godly characteristics or practices. Nowhere is this more poignantly asserted than in the scripture that summarizes the ultimate sacrifice by God in John 3:16: *"For God so loved the world that He gave us His only begotten Son..."* We often quote this verse without much afterthought, or forethought for that matter, taking it for granted as God's demonstration of His love and as a means of reconciliation between God and humans. We fail to raise the question as to how this can, and must, be reflected in our own manner of living. By linking this divine sacrifice to our own giving, among other things, Cynthia Paintsil illustrates the inviolability of giving, for we are called to give because God gives. Such demonstration of the principle of giving would suffice in and of itself. But she does more to unpack the various forms of giving and their scriptural basis, as well as the reasons for each form of giving. In this excellent book, we learn about firstfruits, tithes, free will offerings, and alms.

Drawing from both the Old Testament and the New Testament, this revelatory book expatiates on the enduring principles of these forms of giving and debunks the fallacies of outmodedness with which so many often approach these principles. Cynthia Paintsil also draws from her own experiences and the application of these principles to her life. These personal narratives are precious gems, illustrating the practicality of giving and affirming its personally transforming nature. The prayer at the end of the book brings everything together in a succinct manner with words to be used as a prayer, read aloud, and meditated upon.

--

Benjamin Kwakye, BA (Dartmouth), JD (Harvard), is lead counsel at a multinational company. He is a board member of the Africa Education Initiative. Kwakye is also a multiple award-winning novelist and poet.   Among his awards are the ALA Book of the Year Award for Creative Writing, the regional Commonwealth Writers Prize for Best First Book and Best Book, the IPPY Gold Award for Adult Multicultural Fiction, and an Illumination Book Award for Poetry.

INTRODUCTION

It was the winter of January 2021. The Chicago land and the Midwest region of the U.S.A were in a deep freeze. We had had snowfalls of several inches deep. At the time of writing, we had between 18 to 32 inches of snow on the ground. This was over a period of two weeks. The good news was that the two Sundays sandwiched between these weeks didn't have snowfalls, and the highways and some of the byways had been plowed so we could still drive to church.

Oh yes, I also need to remind you that at this time, we were still in the pandemic of the COVID-19, and once again, the good news was that vaccines had been developed and approved for emergency usage, and as such, mass vaccinations were going on not only in the U.S. but also around the world. What a time it was to be alive in the world!

It was during this period that as a pastor, as always, I was to minister on a Sunday when I received the word of God I'm about to share with you during my preparation. The year had begun with the theme, "The season of Godliness." The main scripture was from 1Timothy 3:16 (NKJV) – *"And without controversy great is the mystery of godliness: God was manifested in the flesh, justified in the Spirit, seen by angels, preached among the Gentiles, believed on in the world, received up in glory."* Other corresponding scriptures that came into play were 1 Timothy 4:7-8, which exhorts us to exercise godliness - *"But reject profane and old wives' fables, and exercise yourself toward godliness. For bodily exercise profits a little, but godliness is profitable for all things, having promise of the life that now is and of that which is to come."* and 1 Timothy 6:11 which also exhorts us to pursue godliness - *"But you, O man of God, flee these things and pursue righteousness, godliness, faith, love, patience, gentleness."*

Now the question is, how does one pursue godliness? Godliness, simply put, is acting like the gods or becoming like a god. For the Christian and, for that matter, a child of God, it involves manifesting a Christ-like nature, the essence of "Christ manifested in the flesh". The revelations from the scripture that came alive to me through the Holy Spirit as our senior pastor taught us and what I also received directly were that we ought to be Christ-like by receiving and having "The Word," which is Christ in us. I had the opportunity to minister a sermon on exercising

2

ourselves unto godliness by having the Word of God abide in us. I also prepared a sermon on "Praying as exercising ourselves onto godliness." Then at the beginning of the year, as I was preparing to minister, God brought to my attention to minister on the first fruits. That was when I asked myself what firstfruits had to do with exercising ourselves unto godliness. The Holy Spirit opened my eyes to see that giving was such a great spiritual activity that transcends the natural and that in our giving, we are exercising ourselves unto godliness and pursuing godliness.

In giving, we are becoming like God because that is His nature. God was the first person who gave of Himself to us. For scripture says in John 3:16, one of the most popular bible verses, *"For God so loved the world that He gave His only begotten Son, that whoever believes in Him should not perish but have everlasting life."* He took the form of man, manifested in the flesh as the second person of the trinity, died for us, rose up, and became the first fruits of many as seen in 1Corinthians 15:20 *"But now Christ is risen from the dead, and has become the firstfruits of those who have fallen asleep."* What a mind-boggling knowledge and revelation! As I prepared my sermon, I was so excited and thrilled about

3

the enormity of the revelation God had given to me and I believe the Lord spoke to me that I was not only going to preach that sermon on that day but I was going to preach it in one of our other church campuses. I wasn't sure how that was going to play out though. The plan was to call the resident pastor of that campus to let him know that I would like to come over the next Sunday to preach. Interestingly, I didn't follow through with the call as the days rolled by and guess what, that weekend, we were snowed in once again. We couldn't go for church services. Every campus had a virtual service on Zoom. So I told myself that it was not God's plan for me to minister that sermon on that campus after all. Little did I know that it was still God's plan. The week after, interestingly enough, the pastor of that campus gave me a call that I should come over and minister. I had made plans that very week he wanted me to minister and I told him I would do so the following week.

As I prayed and prepared, I told myself that I had to preach on a different sermon other than giving since our Harvest/ First Fruit and Thanksgiving service had been held two weeks prior. The more I prayed, the less headway I had with any topic to minister on. Interestingly enough, the Holy Spirit started giving me more insights into the topic of "giving" as exercising ourselves unto godliness. I had more insights into the free-will offering, alms, tithes and firstfruits offering. However, I was still determined that it was not an appropriate topic for that time. I woke up the Sunday morning with nothing to preach on, and funny enough, I was still thinking of preaching on something else besides giving.

Finally, it was as if the Holy Spirit was not asking me but screaming at me to do His will and not mine, and that was to preach the message on" giving." I just took the message as it was from the previous sermon, and God asked me to minister the same sermon. Then it all came to me how I had known, and I believed God had told me that I was going to preach that same message at that campus. You can't believe the liberty, peace, and utterance I had as I ministered that Sunday. It was like every statement I made was divinely inspired. Well, I believe I heard from God that the next step was to share this inspiration with the entire world. It is not because this message has never been preached before, certainly not, but because God always does something new with His word each time He inspires it. He gives fresh ideas and revelations to the same scripture over and over again, just as His mercies and grace are renewed every morning. Once again, tighten your seatbelts as we take a journey to explore giving as exercising ourselves unto godliness. I trust that you'll be immensely blessed, and please share this book and message with many others.

Chapter 1

Giving Is A Spiritual Activity

"For God so loved the world that He gave His only begotten Son, that whoever believes in Him should not perish but have everlasting life."
John 3:16

Every form of giving has a significant spiritual root, and that root is Jesus Christ. The greatest gift ever given is God giving of Himself to mankind in the form of the second person of the Trinity, Jesus Christ, the begotten Son of the Father. Scripture tells us in John 3:16 that - *"For God so loved the world that He gave His only begotten Son, that whoever believes in Him should not perish but have everlasting life."*

Giving started with God. That is His nature. The history of mankind begins with God creating mankind in His own image and likeness. As if that was not enough, God blessed them and gave them a divine mandate as seen in Genesis1:26-28: *"Then God said, "Let Us make man in Our image, according to Our likeness; let them have dominion over the fish of the sea, over the birds of the air, and over the cattle, over all the earth and over every creeping thing that creeps on the earth." So God created man in His own image; in the image of God, He created him; male and female He created them. Then God blessed them, and God said to them, "Be fruitful and multiply; fill the earth and subdue it; have dominion over the fish of the sea, over the birds of the air, and over every living thing that moves on the earth."* The blessing of God is the divine enablement or what is also referred to as grace, to carry out the divine mandate to be fruitful, multiply, subdue and have dominion. What a loving God! He never gives you an assignment without giving the necessary provisions to carry it out.

God continued His giving spree as He gave to mankind everything that he will have need of on the earth to make him comfortable, to be nourished and cherished as seen in Genesis 1:29-30, "And God said, *"See, I have given you every herb that yields seed which is on the face of all the earth, and every tree whose fruit yields seed; to you, it shall be for food. Also, to every beast of the earth, to every bird of the air, and to everything that creeps on the earth, in which there is life, I have given every green herb for food," and it was so."* This is the nature of our God, and as one hymn writer puts it, "He gives and gives again." Yes, and up until now, God continues to give to us again and again. This provision of God for mankind is still available. Unfortunately, some people do not experience it because they do not tap into His grace. God knows our needs, and He freely gives us all things to enjoy! Right after creation, mankind fell by sinning against God in disobedience to His command in Genesis 3:17a *"Then to Adam He said, "Because you have heeded the voice of your wife, and have eaten from the tree of which I commanded you, saying, 'You shall not eat of it."* But guess what? God had already made a plan of redemption for mankind even before the earth was formed, and that involved the giving of Himself through the lamb that was slain from the foundation of the earth as seen in Revelations 13:8b *"... whose names have not been written in the Book of Life of the Lamb slain from the foundation of the world."*

Due to God's obsession with us and His great love for us, at a time when man's heart was continually evil, He preserved a righteous lineage for Himself. He chose and called Abraham and blessed him, and not only that but also through him, all the nations of the earth was to be blessed. We see this in Genesis 12:1-3: *"Now the LORD had said to Abram: "Get out of your country, from your family and from your father's house, to a land that I will show you. I will make you a great nation; I will bless you and make your name great; and you shall be a blessing. I will bless those who bless you, and I will curse him who curses you; and in you, all the families of the earth shall be blessed."* Once again, God comes to the scene and dishes out unimaginable blessings on Abraham and makes him a source and conduit of blessing to all the families of the earth.

However, in the process of time, God asked Abraham to offer unto Him his only and beloved son, Isaac as seen in Genesis 22:2 *"Then He said, "Take now your son, your only son Isaac, whom you love, and go to the land of Moriah, and offer him there as a burnt offering on one of the mountains of which I shall tell you."* Was it necessary for God to have asked Abraham for such an offering?

This is the same question sometimes you and I ask if it is necessary for God to ask us to give Him any kind of offering since He is the possessor of heaven and earth. Well, from the scriptures in Genesis 22:12-13, we realize the deep spiritual significance of Abraham's offering. *"And He said, "Do not lay your hand on the lad, or do anything to him; for now I know that you fear God, since you have not withheld your son,*

10

your only son, from Me. Then Abraham lifted his eyes and looked, and there behind him was a ram caught in a thicket by its horns. So Abraham went and took the ram, and offered it up for a burnt offering instead of his son." Firstly, God did not take Isaac but gave him back to Abraham. Secondly, God Himself made provision of a lamb for the offering, and that was when Abraham introduced us to God as the God who provides "Jehovah Jireh." Hence, it was not even about the offering per se, but the heart of obedience unto God, causing God to say that "now I know." So you see, it is not about our physical giving.

It is more so of our obedience to God when it comes to our giving or offering. Thus in our giving, God brings us to a place of obedience to Him so that He can testify of us as He did of Abel and also of Abraham. Can God testify of you and me? Our giving is ultimately about trusting in God or having faith in Him. Abraham gave to God because of his faith in Him. We see from scripture in Hebrews 11:17-19 that *"By faith Abraham, when he was tested, offered up Isaac, and he who had received the promises offered up his only begotten son, of whom it was said, "In Isaac your seed shall be called," concluding that God was able to raise him up, even from the*

11

dead, from which he also received him in a figurative sense."
Abraham believed that God is able to raise him (Isaac) from
the dead. You may think he was crazy. Having trusted in God
and waited for so many years until the age of 100 before Isaac
was born, then trusting that God was going to raise Isaac back
to life after he had sacrificed him? Yes, Abraham did, and
that is why scripture says God tested him, and he passed.

His success didn't come from the blue sky or out of nowhere.
It came as a result of knowing that God is able to fulfill all
that He promises. He had had experiences with God and
knew that He never fails. This is what is meant by pursuing
godliness, which is coming to a relationship and fellowship with
God based primarily on faith through the knowledge of Him.
We can also see that the lamb given by God to Abraham
and slain on Mount Moriah is a great spiritual allegory of
what was to come. It represented God's provision of Jesus
Christ for us. Jesus became the Lamb of God that was slain
for the redemption of the world. Thus, if we can believe
and accept this truth that God offered His only son, Jesus
Christ, for us, then just as Abraham believed God, which
was accounted as righteousness, then we can be accounted
as righteous because of our faith. In Galatians 3:26 and 29,

scripture says that *"For you are all sons of God through faith in Christ Jesus. And if you are Christ's, then you are Abraham's seed, and heirs according to the promise."* Now we have come to a full cycle of God's greatest gift to us, Jesus Christ, summarizing the deep spiritual essence of our giving. Is it then a big thing that we give back to God, which is in essence, giving back to ourselves? Absolutely not! God expects us to do so. Sometimes He commands us to do so, and sometimes He gives us our own will to choose to give.

It is very important to note that every sacrifice, given in accordance with God's expectation through faith, ceases to be natural but becomes a spiritual offering. Remember, God is a Spirit, and those who worship Him must worship Him in Spirit and in truth. Our offering, giving, sacrifice, and the like are our worship unto God, and we must always do so by faith. Scripture says in Hebrews 11:6 that "But without faith, it is impossible to please Him, for he who comes to God must believe that He is and that He is a rewarder of those who diligently seek Him." With this understanding, we realize how important our giving is and how we can't deem it lightly by offering just anything to God. It is of an eternal and great spiritual significance.

We have also seen that giving is the nature of God, thus when we give, we are becoming like God and His nature is being reflected in us. There is an Akan proverb that says, "a crab does not give birth to a bird." So it is, that as children of God, created in His image and likeness, we must be like Him and must therefore be giving. There are different forms of giving, and every one of them is deeply rooted in God. There is the giving of the firstfruits and the tithes, which are clear commandments from God. There is then the freewill offering and alms which we are given the choice to give. We will explore these individually in the next chapters. It is interesting that God chooses to judge us not on the giving He demands or expects us to, but on the ones that He gives us our free will to do.

Remember once again that giving is of God. It started with Him, and as we practice it, not only do we display His character and become like Him, but our giving ultimately goes to Him. Hence, just as He gives to us, we also give back to Him, and the unending cycle of giving continues as we share deep fellowship with Him.

Chapter 2

The First Fruits – A More Excellent Sacrifice

"By faith Abel offered to God a more excellent sacrifice than Cain, through which he obtained witness that he was righteous, God testifying of his gifts; and through it he being dead still speaks."
Hebrews 11:4

Firstfruits in the Old Testament

The scripture in Hebrew 11:4, which says that *"By faith, Abel offered to God a more excellent sacrifice than Cain, through which he obtained witness that he was righteous, God testifying of his gifts; and through it he being dead still speaks"* is filled with deep spiritual truths. The full comprehension of it is mind-boggling. Since I was granted a deeper understanding by the Holy Spirit concerning this scripture, I've been wondering how it was possible for me to have read this piece of scripture again and again without getting the full revelation of it. This scripture describes Abel's sacrifice as "a more excellent sacrifice." The description of it as an excellent sacrifice alone could have sufficed, but to have the adverb "more" pre-modify it implies that it was beyond an excellent sacrifice. This is where I was intrigued and decided to title this book as such, even though it talks about other forms of giving.

Now the question is what made this sacrifice earn this description? Why a more excellent sacrifice? Well, interesting enough, the answers are in the subsequent sentences of the same verse. The scripture proceeded to say that, "through which he obtained witness that he was righteous." It means that the sacrifice he offered was a proof of his righteousness. In essence, his sacrifice showed that he had a right standing with God. Not only that but, in the same sentence, we are told that "God testifying of his gifts" -in that God was witness to and approved of Abel's gifts. However, the most exciting and thrilling part of the offering is that "and through it he being dead still speaks." Yes, you read right, that through that sacrifice, Abel is still speaking even as you are reading now! The obvious question on your mind right now must be "how is it possible for someone who is dead to be still speaking?" The answer to this question simply put is that "it was an eternal or spiritual sacrifice."

16

It is a sacrifice that transcends the natural realm into the spiritual realm and continues forever in the presence of God.

Now concerning this more excellent sacrifice, let's go to the beginning to know exactly what it was and how it was offered, as seen in Genesis 4:1 - 5. *"Now Adam knew Eve, his wife, and she conceived and bore Cain, and said, "I have acquired a man from the LORD." Then she bore again, this time his brother Abel. Now Abel was a keeper of sheep, but Cain was a tiller of the ground. And in the process of time, it came to pass that Cain brought an offering of the fruit of the ground to the LORD. Abel also brought of the firstborn of his flock and of their fat. And the LORD respected Abel and his offering, but He did not respect Cain and his offering. And Cain was very angry, and his countenance fell."* First, we realize that both men, Cain and Abel brought an offering to the Lord. Second, God respected Abel and his offering, but God did not respect Cain and his offering. Now the question is, why didn't God respect Cain and his offering? Was there any difference between both offerings?

Absolutely yes,   there was a difference. If we carefully read the   scripture again, we realize that Cain brought an offering of the fruit of the ground, and Abel brought "the firstborn of his flock and of their fat". It makes sense that obviously, a tiller of the ground will offer fruits of the ground and a keeper of sheep will offer flock. Therefore, rightfully speaking, God should have understood, of which I believe He knew and did. But, there was something that differentiated the offering of both men. Abel's offering was not described as "an offering of a sheep from his flock." If that were so, then it would have obviously paralleled that of Cain's. However, Abel's was described as "the firstborn of his flock" and beyond that, the descriptive phrase "and of their fat." This is the stark difference between the two offerings.

So if Abel knew or had the instinct to give of his firstborn flock and their fat thereof to God, why didn't Cain do so? Is it possible that he knew it but decided that he could just give any fruit of the ground to God as an offering? I'm inclined to believe that he did because in the preceding verse in Genesis 4:6-7, *"So the LORD said to Cain, "Why are you angry? And why has your countenance fallen? If you do well, will you not be accepted? And if you do not do well, sin lies at the door. And its desire is for you, but you should rule over it."* Here, God was implying that Cain knew the right thing to do, and not only that, God gave him an opportunity to do so. God gave him a second chance but unfortunately, he didn't take advantage of it, and it became a sin unto him. Remember what was said of Abel in Hebrews 11:4, that his offering was a witness of his righteousness? Abel knew what was right, and he did so; thus, it pleased God. God did not only accept his offering but respected it and respected him.

Why was the firstling or the first fruit so important to God? Why was it the big game-changer when it came to the offering of both men? What is the firstling or, for that matter, the firstfruit? We are given clear and poignant answers in Exodus 13:1-2, 12-13 *"Then the LORD spoke to Moses, saying, "Consecrate to Me all the firstborn, whatever opens the womb among the children of Israel, both of man and beast; it is Mine."* and *"that you shall set apart to the LORD all that open the womb, that is, every firstborn that comes from an animal which you have; the males shall be the LORD's. But every firstborn of a donkey you shall redeem with a lamb; and if you will not redeem it, then you shall break its neck. And all the firstborn of man among your sons you shall redeem."* From the above scripture, this was the time when God had delivered the children of Israel from captivity and bondage in Egypt. They were journeying in the wilderness en-route

19

to the Promised Land. This is where God unveiled His expectations to them. These became their laws, ordinances, and commandments. Prominent among them was to consecrate or set aside all the firstborn, whatever opens the womb among man or beast unto the Lord because they belong to Him. Thus, the "firsts" is always God's. No one is to take that which belongs to Him. Did this apply only to man and beasts? What about the fruit of the ground?

The Lord required of the children of Israel to observe the Feast of the Harvest, the first fruits, as seen in Exodus 23:16 *"and the Feast of Harvest, the firstfruits of your labors which you have sown in the field; and the Feast of Ingathering at the end of the year when you have gathered in the fruit of your labors from the field."* They were also instructed what to do at the time, and that was to offer the first of their first fruits of the land to God as seen in verse 19a: *"The first of the firstfruits of your land you shall bring into the house of the LORD your God."* Thus, the principle of the "firsts" belonging to God also applied to the fruit of the ground. This is why God was displeased with Cain. Cain really had some audacity to flout the expectation of God given that he had the opportunity and a second chance to make it right after

20

he and his offering had been rejected. Rather he was angry, and as God clearly predicted that sin was lying at his door, he plotted and killed his brother. What a double loss for him!

The importance of the Firstlings and Firstfruits cannot be emphasized enough. It was reiterated in the renewal of God's covenant with the Children of Israel. I guess redundancy is the name of the game if you want to affirm the importance of a matter. Thus in Exodus 34:19, 22, and 26a, we see the obvious once again. *"All that open the womb are Mine, and every male firstborn among your livestock, whether ox or sheep." "And you shall observe the Feast of Weeks, of the firstfruits of wheat harvest, and the Feast of Ingathering at the year's end,"* and *"The first of the firstfruits of your land you shall bring to the house of the LORD your God."*

We cannot take these ordinances of God for granted, given the importance attached to them. The firstborn of every man and livestock is God's. Not only that, the first of the firstfruits of the land should be given to Him as well. In the days of the prophets in Ezekiel, when the children of Israel had sinned against God and had been taken into captivity, their elders decided to inquire of the Lord. The Lord was angry with them, and reminded them of all their sins in forsaking His ordinances and statutes. However, He promised them restoration, and accompanying this promise of restoration was a strong requirement of their offerings and the firstfruits of their sacrifices, as seen in Ezekiel 20:40. *"For on My holy mountain, on the mountain height of Israel,"* says the Lord GOD, *"there all the house of Israel, all of them in the land, shall serve Me; there I will accept them, and there I will require your offerings and the firstfruits of your sacrifices, together with all your holy things."* The firstfruits and other offerings are requirements of the Lord, and He takes great delight in them.

A requirement is a thing that is compulsory, a necessary condition that must be satisfied; thus, the firstfruits cannot be ignored but must be offered in order to continue or have that desired relationship and fellowship with God. The offerings and the firstfruit sacrifices went beyond requirements; they were also for restoration and blessing. In Ezekiel 44:30, *"The best of all firstfruits of any kind, and every sacrifice of any kind from all your sacrifices, shall be the priest's; also you shall give to the priest the first of your ground meal, to cause a blessing to rest on your house."* The priesthood had no inheritance. The Lord was their inheritance. The people were instructed to give the firstfruits to them in God's stead, and here, we are made to understand and given a deeper revelation that the purpose of it is to cause a blessing to abide upon one's house. It brings permanency of God's covenant of blessing to His people.

Firstfruits in the New Testament

In 1Corinthians 15:20-23, Apostle Paul explains to the Christians in Corinth at the time how Jesus Christ died and rose up and has become the firstfruits of all who die in Him. *"But now Christ is risen from the dead and has become the firstfruits of those who have fallen asleep. For since by man came death, by Man also came the resurrection of the dead. For as in Adam all die, even so in Christ all shall be made alive. But each one in his own order: Christ the firstfruits, afterward those who are Christ's at His coming."* God never gives us a principle to abide by which He doesn't abide by Himself even though He is the creator and we are His creatures. He has certain expectations of us, which are rightly so because He practices them. Jesus Christ, the second person of the Trinity, the begotten of the Father, the Word, took the form of a man, became flesh, dwelt among us, and

23

was offered unto God on our behalf as the perfect or "a more excellent sacrifice". Hence, through this sacrifice, which became the firstfruits of many to come, we have eternal life. He was God's excellent offering for us. It is therefore not surprising that as the Father is, so must we be and hence, the requirement of us to offer unto Him our firstfruits.

In Romans 8:23, the scripture says that *"Not only that, but we also who have the firstfruits of the Spirit, even we ourselves groan within ourselves, eagerly waiting for the adoption, the redemption of our body"*. We realize that Christ was not the only firstfruit unto God, but there were many to come and that we have also become firstfruits unto God, waiting for the adoption and redemption of our bodies. In James 1:18, scripture clearly confirms this truth that, *"Of His own will He brought us forth by the word of truth, that we might be a kind of firstfruits of His creatures."* This gives us a clear indication that the principle of the firstfruits transcends the natural realm and that it is a highly spiritual ordinance. We have to understand and come to the realization that offering our firstfruits unto God is beyond a natural thing. Once again, it is a deeply spiritual ordinance initiated by God Himself before the world came into existence, as clearly demonstrated in Revelations 13:8b, *"the Book of Life of the Lamb slain from the foundation of the world,"* and clearly, the principle of the firstfruits will continue through into eternity. It is neither an Old Testament nor a New Testament principle, and as such, we must adhere to and practice this principle of God in our lifetime.

Another important aspect of offering our firstfruits unto God is that we are assured that whatever is left for us after we have offered our "firsts" is hallowed and sanctified. In Romans 11:16, the scripture says that *"For if the firstfruit is holy, the lump is also holy; and if the root is holy, so are the branches."* After we have given God His portion of the firstfruits, whatever remains as our portion has the blessing of God upon it. The permanence of God's blessing comes into effect because we offered Him the firstfruits. Why will anyone want to take God's portion and disobey Him? Why would anyone want to miss out on such a blessing and become like Cain, who ended up not only missing out on the blessing but being cursed as well? It's about time we started practicing the principle of the firstfruits in order to receive the permanency of God's blessings in all our endeavors.

Did you know that an acceptable way of honoring God is by the giving of our firstfruits? We will read further on honoring God in Chapter 6 of this book, but while we are on the topic of firstfruits, I will briefly touch on it. In Proverbs 3:9-10, scripture says that *"Honor the LORD with your possessions, And with the firstfruits of all your increase; So your barns will be filled with plenty, And your vats will overflow with new wine."* What a privilege it is to be given an opportunity to honor God by offering our firstfruits! If we are not inclined at all to give our firstfruits to God for any reason, for the sake of honoring God, let's do so because this is the way He has chosen to be honored. Not only that, but just looking at the corresponding blessing alone tells us that it is not about the money, substance, or material thing we give, but God seeking our honor because He gives back to us more than we offer to Him. Let's honor God!

This principle of the firstfruits is very critical and essential in our relationship and fellowship with God. As we read from the beginning, not only does the firstfruits belong to God, He requires them of us, and it also becomes our means of honoring Him. No wonder Abel's offering is still speaking! He honored God, and God was pleased with him and the sacrifice. It was an acceptable offering unto God. Indeed, a blessing of abundance, plenty, and overflowing emanate from pleasing the Lord. Having known these truths from the word of God, is it possible for anyone who is a child of God and a true Christian not to offer their firstfruits unto God? Just do it. Having said all that I can from the biblical perspective, let me share with you my personal story on how I connected into the firstfruits vision, and it became part of my life.

My Personal Story

Growing up in the church, I had heard and understood the principle of tithes, offering, and alms but not of the firstfruits. I read about it in scriptures and perhaps, heard it mentioned by preachers, but all along, I always thought the firstfruits and tithes were the same thing. It was not until one day, when one of our associate pastors ministered at church, that he zeroed in on the firstfruits, indicating it was a different principle from the tithe. Even at that time, I couldn't fully grasp the concept until my husband and Senior Pastor started teaching on it. He had also been of the same belief until then.

We, from then onwards, decided to obey this principle of God and started giving our firstfruits. We always tremble at the word of God and always hearken and obey it. One principle I hold dear to my heart is that I will obey God in error than to disobey God in ignorance, which will be a great folly.

Having understood the principle of the firstfruits, I realized that I had practiced it unknowingly. Something inherently told me that I had to give my very first paycheck out as a sacrifice unto God. Now I know that "that something" within me that was speaking to me was the voice of the Holy Spirit, which is one of the primary ways through which God speaks to us. So, in essence, God spoke to me, and I'm glad I obeyed. I remember growing up, when I finished my secondary school education, I had to do my "National Service" - (This was when you were assigned to a school, an organization, etc. to work for the nation for one year before you continued your education to the tertiary level or University). Fortunately, I was posted to a school in my community. To make a long story short, when I received my first paycheck, I took my younger brother to a store and bought him whatever he wanted, paid my tithes, and whatever was left, I found a way to give out. In essence, that entire paycheck had become a kind of firstfruit. I knew it was not mine, so I couldn't spend it on me but had to give it all out as a sacrifice unto God.

Not only that, when I came to the U.S. to join my husband, a good friend of ours brought her daughter to me to take care of while she went to school. At the time, I was home and preparing to write my GMAT, GRE, etc., to go to graduate school. I wasn't expecting any form of payment from her until she surprised me one day with some money as an appreciation for babysitting her daughter. That was the very first time I had earned any income since I came to the U.S. Guess what? My first instinct was to be a blessing to someone because, innately, I realized that money was hallowed. I knew I couldn't use that money for myself even though there were so many things I could have done with it. By God's grace, I obeyed that inner voice and gave that money away. I was a blessing to someone who was in need but also working very hard in the kingdom. Yes, once again, I had given my first fruits of the land to God without even knowing it.

This experience, I believe, is not peculiar to me alone. I know that my husband has had such experiences as well. He gave out his first earnings to be a blessing to others and the church without knowing that he was following the principle of the firstfruits. I'm sure there are others who have had such experiences.

Well, this should not come as a surprise. The word of God says that in the dispensation of the Holy Spirit, which is our time now, He'll write His laws in our hearts so that we will not sin against Him. He'll lead us by His Spirit, and He'll teach us. No wonder we are able to do the will of God without any formal lessons or teachings on the firstfruits. To God be the glory! I want you to be challenged to do the bidding of God. Do not harden your heart when you hear the voice of the Spirit of God speak to you and direct you. As has been my maxim, I'd rather obey God in error than to disobey in ignorance.

Giving our Firstfruits

The question is, how do we know what our firstfruits are, and how do we give them since we are not in the agrarian culture? Well, I believe that the first salary or income we receive becomes our firstfruits. It could be that of the first week, the first two weeks, or the first month. It depends on what God tells us and what we find comfortable doing. Also, at the beginning of every year, we have to choose that time to give our firstfruits to God. Remember that the children of Israel had to do it at the beginning of every harvest, so it wasn't a once-in-a-lifetime principle. It was an annual or seasonal principle. Thus, in our modern-day, the beginning of our year becomes the best time to do so.

When it comes to who or where to give the firstfruits, clearly God instructed that it be given to the priest as seen in Ezekiel 44:30, *"The best of all firstfruits of any kind, and every sacrifice of any kind from all your sacrifices shall be the priest's; also you shall give to the priest the first of your ground meal, to cause a blessing to rest on your house."* If we belong to a local body of Christ, we have to offer it there. You have to put it in an envelope, label it as the firstfruits, and put it in the offering bowl or tray. In recent times, with our virtual services and online giving, you can send it to the church's account by labeling it as such in the memo. We are not to give our firstfruits as gifts or charity as I did when I did not have the knowledge or understanding. It must be given to the priest through the church. Gifts and charity or alms have their place as far as giving is concerned. If you do not belong to any church or local body of Christ, I believe there is still a church or minister of God who has been a blessing to you or others; thus, do well to send your firstfruits to them as God's representatives, and as you obey God's principle to the fullest, you will reap its fullest blessing as well.

Let us not be deceived by those who claim it is an Old Testament principle. Clearly, from the word of God, we've realized that it was practiced by Abel before the law was set in place. It was made clear in the law and was practiced by Moses and the children of Israel. Thereafter, Christ Himself became God's firstfruits. It is a spiritual and an eternal phenomenon. Don't be left out.

Honor God with your firstfruits so that your bank accounts will never be empty and you'll have the endless provision of God. Most importantly, like Abel, as you give your firstfruits, may it continually speak on your behalf, show your righteousness, and may God be pleased with you and your sacrifice, and may it become a "more excellent sacrifice" in the sight of God.

Chapter 3

The Tithe

"Bring all the tithes into the storehouse, that there may be food in My house, and try Me now in this," Says the LORD of hosts, "If I will not open for you the windows of heaven and pour out for you such blessing that there will not be room enough to receive it."
Malachi 3:10

As Christians, many of us have heard of the word "tithes" without knowing exactly what it is, or we may just have a vague idea or an understanding of it. The simple present-day definition of the tithe is 10% of your income/earnings given for the support of the church and clergy. This is a divine ordinance that has been in existence since God introduced Himself to man. From the word of God, it was practiced during the time of Abraham, before the law was given to the children of Israel. It became part of the law, and after the law, in the dispensation of Jesus Christ, He spoke about it while addressing the Pharisees and Sadducees, and in the dispensation of the Holy Spirit, in which we presently are, the

Apostle Paul gave a great insight into this divine ordinance.

Tithing was practiced in the dispensation of the Father, that is, the days or times when the first person of the Trinity or Godhead communicated directly with men as individuals, prophets, kings, and priests. Also, in the dispensation of the Son, Jesus Christ, the practice continued, and Jesus actually affirmed the paying of tithes while condemning other religious practices at the time. When Jesus had ascended to heaven, and the dispensation of the Holy Spirit came, Apostle Paul received the divine revelation into tithing, bringing us to the realization of how deeply spiritual tithing is. Thus, proceeding from here, we will look at tithing before, during, and after the law to establish its deep spiritual and divine essence.

Tithing before the Law

In the book of Genesis 14: 14-24, we are told how Abraham and Melchizedek met and the former paid tithes to the latter. This was the first time we heard of tithing in the scriptures. *"Now when Abram heard that his brother was taken captive, he armed his three hundred and eighteen trained servants who were born in his own house, and went in pursuit as far* as Dan. He divided his forces against them by night, and he and his servants attacked them and pursued them as far as Hobah, which is north of Damascus. So he brought back all the goods, and also brought back his brother Lot and his goods, as well as the women and the people. And the king of Sodom went out to meet him at the Valley of Shaveh (that is, the King's Valley), after his return from the defeat of Chedorlaomer and the kings who were with him. Then Melchizedek king of Salem brought out bread and wine; he was the priest of God Most High. And he blessed him and said: "Blessed be Abram of God Most High, Possessor of heaven and earth; And blessed be God Most High, Who has delivered your enemies into your hand."And he gave him a tithe of all. Now the king of Sodom said to Abram, "Give me the persons, and take the goods for yourself." But Abram said to the king of Sodom, "I have raised my hand to the LORD, God Most High, the Possessor of heaven and earth, that I will take nothing, from a thread to a sandal strap, and that I will not take anything that is yours, lest you should say, 'I have made Abram rich'— except only what the young men have eaten, and the portion of the men who went with me: Aner, Eshcol, and Mamre; let them take their portion."

From the above scripture reading, we learn of how Abram

took men of his household to pursue men who had taken his nephew Lot and other people captive. Abram brought back his brother Lot and his goods, as well as the women and the people and all the goods that had been taken from them. Suddenly, we are introduced to Melchizedek, king of Salem, who was the priest of God Most High. He met with Abram, brought out bread and wine, and I'm assuming he shared it with Abram, and scripture says that he blessed him. During the encounter, we are told that Abram "gave him a tithe of all."

I am sure the first question that comes to mind is, "who was this Melchizedek?" Thank God the Apostle Paul gave us some answers, which we will look at that under Tithing after the law. In the meantime, the poignant thing here to learn is that Abram gave him tithes of all that he had obtained from his conquest. Why did Abram do so? Was it an innate thing in him that told him to do so? Did he know that it was an ordinance of God? Was it the practice at the time? Whatever or whichever the answers were, he knew he had to do so, and most importantly, he did, and he received a blessing from Melchizedek. One thing of note here is that Melchizedek said it was the Most High God who had delivered Abram's enemies into his hands. Thus, his victory was not gotten by his own strength but by the divine intervention of God. This knowledge alone required that Abraham give the due acknowledgment, thanks and honor to God, and no wonder he gave tithes of all that he had acquired to the priest of the Most High God.

Also, before the law in Genesis 28:10-22, we are told that Jacob vowed to God to give Him his tithes if He blessed him after a divine encounter. *"Now Jacob went out from Beersheba and went toward Haran. So he came to a certain place and stayed there all night because the sun had set. And he took one of the stones of that place and put it at his head, and he lay down in that place to sleep. Then he dreamed, and behold, a ladder was set up on the earth, and its top reached to heaven, and there the angels of God were ascending and descending on it. And behold, the LORD stood above it and said: "I am the LORD God of Abraham your father and the God of Isaac; the land on which you lie I will give to you and your descendants. Also, your descendants shall be as the dust of the earth; you shall spread abroad to the west and the east, to the north and the south; and in you and in your seed all the families of the earth shall be blessed. Behold, I am with you and will keep you wherever you go and will bring you back to this land, for I will*

not leave you until I have done what I have spoken to you."
Then Jacob awoke from his sleep and said, "Surely the
LORD is in this place, and I did not know it." And he was
afraid and said, "How awesome is this place! This is none
other than the house of God, and this is the gate of heaven!"
Then Jacob rose early in the morning, and took the stone
that he had put at his head, set it up as a pillar, and poured
oil on top of it. And he called the name of that place Bethel,
but the name of that city had been Luz previously. Then
Jacob made a vow, saying, "If God will be with me, and keep
me in this way that I am going, and give me bread to eat
and clothing to put on so that I come back to my father's
house in peace, then the LORD shall be my God. And this
stone which I have set as a pillar shall be God's house, and
of all that You give me I will surely give a tenth to You."

What preceded this story was that Jacob had deceived his father
Isaac and taken the blessing of his older brother Esau. His
brother was very angry with him and was planning to kill
him, so he had to run away. He was on his way to his uncle
Laban's house as he had been instructed by his mother
Rebecca when he had this divine encounter. Can you imagine

a man under such distress of running away from home only to come into such a great encounter with the Almighty God? He was visited in the dream by God, and He rehashed the promises he had made to his grandfather Abraham and his father Isaac to him. He woke up from the dream and knew he had encountered God as he said, *"How awesome is this place! This is none other than the house of God, and this is the gate of heaven!"* He took the stone he laid his head on and poured oil on it, and made a vow to God that if God will make provision for him and bring him back to his home safely, he will build a house for God in that place and not only that but *"of all that You give me I will surely give a tenth to You."* Jacob made a vow to God to pay his tithes to Him.

Once again, the question is why the 10% of all that God will give him? Just like his grandfather Abraham, was it an innate thing in him that told him to do so? Did he know that it was an ordinance of God? Was it the practice at the time? Whatever the answers are, he knew he had to do so; hence, he made that vow unto God. One thing worthy of note here is that just like in Abraham's situation, Jacob knew it was the Most High God who is able to keep him and bless him, and that if he was going to be successful in his journey and return in peace, it would not be by his own strength, but by the divine intervention of God. Once again, just as in the case of Abraham, this knowledge alone required that Jacob gave the due acknowledgment, thanks, and honor to God, and no wonder he vowed to build a house for God and to give tithes of all that he would acquire to the Most High God.

Clearly, we see a pattern unfolding here about the essence of giving tithes, which is the acknowledgment that God is the one who gives us all things, and it is our duty to give thanks and honor that is due Him. Let's take a look at tithing in the law, which will give us further insights into the essence of tithing.

Tithing in the Law

When God delivered the children of Israel from bondage in the land of Egypt as His chosen people, He gave them laws and statutes to abide by. Included in these laws was tithing, as can be seen in Leviticus 27:30 - 32: "And all the tithe of the land, whether of the seed of the land or of the fruit of the tree, is the

LORD's. It is holy to the LORD. If a man wants at all to redeem any of his tithes, he shall add one-fifth to it. And concerning the tithe of the herd or the flock, of whatever passes under the rod, the tenth one shall be holy to the LORD." God made it very clear to them that the tithe was His, and it was holy unto Him. This is what makes it divine. When one was unable to give it at the right time and wanted to redeem it - when they were ready to offer it to the Lord - they had to add one-fifth to it.

I'm sure we are still wondering why we should give tithes to God. Why would God make a law of it? Fortunately, in Numbers 18:21-24, we are given an explanation for it, that the tithes are the portion of the Levites, God's chosen tribe to carry out His work: "Behold, I have given the children of Levi all the tithes in Israel as an inheritance in return for the work which they perform, the work of the tabernacle of meeting. Hereafter, the children of Israel shall not come near the tabernacle of meeting, lest they bear sin and die. But the Levites shall perform the work of *the tabernacle of meeting and they shall bear their iniquity; it shall be a statute forever, throughout your generations, that among the children of Israel they shall have no inheritance. For the tithes of the children of Israel, which they offer up as a heave offering to the LORD, I have given to the Levites as an inheritance; therefore I have said to them, "Among the children of Israel they shall have no inheritance."* The Levites did not have any inheritance on the land. They belonged to God as His inheritance. They did service unto the Lord on behalf of all their brethren. They couldn't do any other work than to serve the Lord; thus, God gave them the tithes of the land as their inheritance for their well-being and for the upkeep of themselves and their families. Thus, the tithes are God's compensation to the Levites or priests for the work they do for Him.

Unlike their brethren when they possessed the Promised Land, they were not assigned any portion where they could cultivate or keep livestock. God had assigned them wholly unto His service. This is why a tenth part of whatever their brethren earned as a result of the increase of their land was to be given to them as God's representatives. This is what has transpired unto this present day. The ministers of God are compensated through our tithes because they have to commit themselves wholly to the service of God. So when we fail as children of God to pay our tithes, we are denying the priests of God what is rightfully theirs. We are asking them to work without any remuneration. God does not take kindly to this; that is why the need for tithing was emphasized numerous times in the law.

When Hezekiah became king, he decided to make things right in Israel because his predecessors had ceased from following the Lord and His statutes. The house of the Lord had been forsaken, and the priests had stopped rendering services to the Lord because they did not have any support. King Hezekiah's initial line of action was to restore the house of the Lord, bring back the priests, and the worship of the Lord. Therefore, he gave a command to this effect as seen in 2 Chronicles 31:4-6 *"Moreover he commanded the people who dwelt in Jerusalem to contribute support for the priests and the Levites, that they might devote themselves to the Law of the LORD. As soon as the commandment was circulated, the children of Israel brought in abundance the firstfruits of grain and wine, oil and honey, and of all the produce of the field; and they brought in abundantly the tithe of everything. And the children of Israel and Judah, who dwelt in the cities of Judah, brought the tithe of oxen and sheep; also the tithe of holy things which were consecrated to the LORD their God they laid in heaps."* The people who dwelt in Jerusalem quickly obeyed the command to contribute to the support of the priests and Levites by bringing in their tithes and firstfruits in abundance. Righteousness was restored upon the land of Judah in the reign of King Hezekiah and the Lord, in turn, blessed them exceedingly. There was a victorious reign of the time, and because of King Hezekiah's heart towards God, like David, God prospered him greatly.

A similar scenario played out in the time of Nehemiah. Nehemiah led the third and last return of the children of Israel to Jerusalem after the Babylonian exile. As always, the children of Israel had sinned against God and forsaken His ways. As a result, God gave them as captives into the hands of their enemies, but because of His sure mercies and covenant with David, He restored them. He gave Nehemiah great favor in the sight of the king of Babylon, and he returned to Jerusalem with provisions to rebuild its broken walls. But beyond this physical restoration was the re-establishment and institution of the Lord's commandments. The most important among them was to return service in the house of the Lord, which had been forsaken. In Nehemiah 10:37-39, they vowed not to forsake the house of the Lord any longer but "to bring the firstfruits of our dough, our offerings, the fruit from all kinds of trees, the new wine and oil, to the priests, to the storerooms of the house of our God; and to bring the tithes of our land to the Levites, for the Levites should receive the tithes in all our farming communities. And the priest, the descendant of Aaron, shall be with the Levites when the Levites receive tithes; and the Levites shall bring up a tenth of the tithes to the house of our God, to the rooms of the storehouse" Returning to the Lord always involved bringing back the priests and Levites to render services to God and His people, and the only way this could be achieved was through the people bringing their tithes and firstfruits for the upkeep of the Levites. The people did so gladly, and in Nehemiah 12:44, we see that they rejoiced over the priests and Levites. *"And at the same time some were appointed over the rooms of the storehouse for the offerings, the firstfruits, and the tithes, to gather into them from the fields of the cities the portions specified by the Law for the priests and Levites; for Judah rejoiced over the priests and Levites who ministered."* Just as the firstfruits are the Lord's and must be set apart for Him, so are the tithes. The tithes are primarily for the upkeep of the ministers of God.

It is very interesting to note a discourse between God and His people through the prophet Malachi on the issue of tithes.

God says that the people have actually robbed Him in not bringing their tithes to the storehouse and left it empty. To rob is to take something from someone by unlawful force or threat of violence. The violence includes inflicting pain and injury. Is not paying your tithes such a serious crime? Yes, it is! God describes those who do not pay their tithes as "robbers." He says so repeatedly in the verses below in Malachi 3:6-12: *"Will a man rob God? For I am the LORD, I do not change; therefore, you are not consumed, O sons of Jacob. Yet from the days of your fathers, you have gone away from My ordinances and have not kept them. Return to Me, and I will return to you," says the LORD of hosts. "But you said, 'In what way shall we return?' Will a man rob God? Yet you have robbed Me! But you say, 'In what way have we robbed You?'" In tithes and offerings. You are cursed with a curse, for you have robbed Me, even this whole nation. Bring all the tithes into the storehouse, That there may be food in My house, And try Me now in this," says the LORD of hosts, "If I will not open for you the windows of heaven And pour out for you such blessing that there will not be room enough to receive it.1 "And I will rebuke the devourer for your sakes, So that he will not destroy the fruit of your ground, nor shall the vine fail to bear fruit for you in the field," says*

the LORD of hosts; "And all nations will call you blessed,
For you will be a delightful land," says the LORD of hosts."

Not paying one's tithes is going away from the Lord's covenant, and it is inevitably going away from the Lord Himself. It simply means that we cannot profess to be children of God and have a relationship or fellowship with Him and not pay our tithes. Not only do we sin by disobeying God's commands and breaking the fellowship, but we also are deemed as robbers by not paying our tithes. What happens to robbers? Obviously, they are prosecuted! As Christians and, for that matter, children of God, when we get to this state, it means that we open ourselves up to the prosecutor-in-chief, who is the devil. Guess what? The devil is not going to play hide and seek with you. His duty is to steal, kill, and destroy you, and he will do so with much glee as you open yourself up to him. God is admonishing us to return to Him by bringing in our tithes to His storehouse so that His ministers may be taken care of. It is more of our actions than our words. Our act of bringing our tithes to God's storehouse is an indication of our obedience to Him and our fellowship with Him. Beyond that, He promises to rebuke the "devourer" who is the devil, from taking away from us, destroying or even killing us. As if that is not enough, God promises to immensely bless us beyond measure; all nations will call us blessed as our blessings will be made obvious. He promises to ".. open for you the windows of heaven And pour out for you such blessing that there will not be room enough to receive it." Finally, we shall be a delightful people. Do we have anything to lose in paying our tithes? Absolutely nothing! Rather, we have much more to gain. So once again, like Nike says, "just do it!"

Tithes after The Law

What then do we say of tithing as mentioned in the New Testament? During the dispensation of God the Son, Jesus Christ, He addressed the issue of the tithes. Jesus condemned the hypocritical practices of the Pharisees and Sadducees of the time. However, in Luke 11:42 and Matthew 23:23, Jesus commended the Pharisees for paying their tithes. *"But woe to you Pharisees! For you tithe mint and rue and all manner of herbs, and pass by justice and the love of God. These you ought to have done without leaving the others undone." "Woe to you, scribes and Pharisees, hypocrites! For you pay tithe of mint and anise and cumin and have neglected the weightier matters of the law: justice and mercy and faith. These you ought to have done, without leaving the others undone"* Clearly, Jesus was saying that indeed the tithing was necessary as indicated in the phrase *"These you ought to have done."* This tells us that giving our tithes is a necessary thing that needs to be done. We cannot take it for granted or assume it is a thing of the past. Once again, like the firstfruits, every principle or ordinance that emanates from God is divine and, as such eternal.

The Apostle Paul gives further credence to this truth under the inspiration of the Holy Spirit. In Hebrews 7:1-10, the Apostle Paul gives us an in-depth revelation on tithes. *"For this Melchizedek, king of Salem, priest of the Most High God, who met Abraham returning from the slaughter of the kings and blessed him, to whom also Abraham gave a tenth part of all, first being translated "king of righteousness," and then also king of Salem, meaning "king of peace," without father, without mother, without genealogy, having neither beginning of days nor end of life, but made like the Son of God, remains a priest continually. Now consider how great this*

49

man was, to whom even the patriarch Abraham gave a tenth of the spoils. And indeed those who are of the sons of Levi, who receive the priesthood, have a commandment to receive tithes from the people according to the law, that is, from their brethren, though they have come from the loins of Abraham; but he whose genealogy is not derived from them received tithes from Abraham and blessed him who had the promises. Now beyond all contradiction, the lesser is blessed by the better. Here mortal men receive tithes, but there he receives them, of whom it is witnessed that he lives. Even Levi, who receives tithes, paid tithes through Abraham, so to speak, for he was still in the loins of his father when Melchizedek met him."

Here, the Apostle Paul takes us back to the beginning where Abraham gave a tenth part of all the spoil he had gathered after the slaughter of the kings to Melchizedek. We are given a little glimpse as to who Melchizedek is. We learn that he is the "king of righteousness" and the king of Salem, meaning "king of peace." We also learn that he is without genealogy: "having neither beginning of days nor end of life". Clearly, this is an immortal being. Paul just falls short of saying that this person is Jesus Christ, but says "made like the Son of

God." Who can be referred to as the king of righteousness apart from Almighty God, who has the covenant name of Jehovah Tsekenu, which means Jehovah our Sanctifier or Righteousness? Also, who can be called the king of peace apart from God Almighty with the covenant name Jehovah Shalom, meaning Jehovah our Peace? Thinking about it, what creature doesn't have beginning of days aside the creator Himself? This brings us to Jesus' own words in – John 8:58 that *"Before Abraham was, I am."* Could it be God himself who met with Abraham at the time? It is not surprising at all since Abraham had encountered God in different fashions. Paul further elaborates the fact that Abraham didn't pay tithes for himself alone but for Levi, who was in his loins then. Levi was four generations away, so how could he also have paid tithes through his great grandfather? This tells us of the eternal purpose of the tithes. When we pay our tithes, it doesn't end with us. It continues to be a blessing to many generations to come. This is huge - such a great revelation! Every parent seeks the welfare of his children and their children, so if not for our sakes, for that of our children and their children, let us commit ourselves to practice this great ordinance of God.

To complete the revelation on tithing, the Apostle Paul

concludes, *"Here mortal men receive tithes, but there he receives them, of whom it is witnessed that he lives."* Upon this revelation, can we still dare to say that tithing is an Old Testament principle? Absolutely not! We understand the statement, *"Here mortal men receive tithes,"* that we give our tithes to the priesthood who are mortal men just as we are, to be used in their upkeep as they render services to God. However, the solemn truth is that the priesthood is receiving the tithes on behalf of God. That is why the scripture says, *"but there he receives them, of whom it is witnessed that he lives."* Remember that the tithes and firstfruits are to be hallowed unto Him. Also, the priesthood is the Lord's inheritance, so whatever is given to them is given in the name of God, and therefore, it becomes God's. The most intriguing part of this revelation is when he says, *"but there he receives them, of whom it is witnessed that he lives."* Where is being referred to as "there"? I believe it is referring to eternity: the place we will go to after we have exited the earthly portals. So Melchizedek or (Jesus Christ Himself – my personal belief) receives us together with our tithes any time we offer it. He lives in a timeless realm, which is why when we pay our tithes, it carries forward to our offspring. This establishes the truth that tithing is indeed a divine institution.

To reiterate what we read from the beginning of this chapter, the tithe is simply 10% of your income/earnings given for the support of the church and clergy for us modern-day Christians, and as such, children of God. Let us do this with joy and gladness in our hearts. As we read from Malachi, the consequences of not paying our tithes are dire, whereas the benefits are amazing and mind-boggling. Once again, like Nike says, just do it!

My Personal Story on the Tithe

I heard of the word 'tithe' in my teenage years. I'll say, perhaps, when I was 14 or 15 years. I'd become born again just prior to starting a boarding junior high school, to be specific, Holy Child School in Cape-Coast Ghana, West Africa. I was a catholic then, but I always visited a charismatic church with my mom. I believe I was convicted of sin, and when the altar call was made for those who wanted to give their life to Christ, I stepped forward and did so. While in school, I attended my Catholic masses regularly, given that the junior high school was a catholic institution, but when we were on breaks, and I came home, I attended the charismatic church with my mom. I believe it was one of these times that I heard a sermon on tithing. I was touched by the word, and I knew that it was the right thing to do. I didn't have any income then, but anytime I received a gift or anything, I paid my tithes on it. I find it interesting that at the time when I received my first salary, I didn't think of paying tithes on it, but had the inclination of giving it all out. I didn't know about the firstfruits then, and little did I know of the significance of what I did. I'm so glad I obeyed the promptings of the Holy Spirit and ended up giving my first fruits to God. Throughout my schooling days into the university, I paid my tithes faithfully on any money I received. What spurred me on and encouraged me most to give my tithe was the giving habit of my mother. She paid her tithes faithfully. She worked at the bank then, and at the end of every week, she'd come home with brand new, fresh smelling money notes set aside for Sunday offerings, tithes, and gifts to bless some individuals God had laid on her heart.

I remember so well that she would put her fresh notes for tithes in an envelope with her name on it and label it tithes when they were due at the end of every month. This she did faithfully every month for years. I also remember clearly the time she retired and couldn't pay tithes since she was not receiving any consistent income, and our senior pastor then commented either directly to me or with my mom in a conversation that they were not seeing my mom's tithes and asked whether everything was all right with us. It was then that we told our Senior Pastor that my mom had retired. We were pleasantly surprised that our pastor knew she was paying her tithes. Our Senior Pastor made a comment that I remember so vividly to this day. "How can anyone miss out on Mrs. Essel's tithes?" He had been informed by the offering center crew how my mom always put in fresh notes in a clean envelope for her tithes and offering. Thus, they always looked forward to her tithes and offerings. He said there were times they actually showed them to him because of how impressive it was presented. Wow! If men could be that impressed, how much more God? This was a giving that was well-prepared, thought through and given unto God from the heart. I also remember my Dad, who then did not have an understanding of the tithe and always complained that my mom was giving all our money to the church. Now, he has come to appreciate that despite his opposition then, my mom didn't listen to him but did what she believed was right. That I believe turned out to be one of the sources of blessing of God upon our family.

Comparing our family before my mom became a born-again Christian and started paying her tithes faithfully to our lives afterward, clearly, in the latter life, the windows of heaven had been opened upon us; the devourer had been rebuked, and we were prospering. We were not the Rockefellers then, but we never lacked; rather, we were a great source of blessing to many around us. The difference was obvious, and God was truly at work in our lives. I am blessed to have met my wonderful husband, and together, we believe crazily in the principle of tithing. My husband is responsible for our finances. We have never and will never miss out on paying our tithes by the grace of God. We do so religiously. There is no other way around paying our tithes. It is a simple principle, and that is giving 10% of our increase to God. Due to our commitment to this divine principle, the Essel (my maiden name) family and the Paintsil family have never lacked. God has always made provision beyond our needs and made us a source of great blessings to many people. True to God's word in Malachi 3:10, *"Bring all the tithes into the storehouse, that there may be food in My house, and try Me now in this,"* says the LORD of hosts, *"If I will not open for you the windows of heaven and pour out for you such blessing that there will not be room enough to receive it,"* we have tried

God and proven Him, and His word has come true in our lives.

To conclude, just take God at his word because He never fails! I've been privileged to be a pastor for all these years and also gotten to know a lot of families who have been faithful in their tithing, and I can testify that they have never lacked but continue to prosper. These faithful families have the rest and peace of God all around them and their children. I've also seen those who have not been so faithful in their tithing and giving in general. You be the judge of their predicament. You can clearly see the work of the devourer in their lives all the time, including cars breaking down, hospital visits, emergencies, and whatnot.

You cannot take the word of God for granted. As He promises in Joshua 1:8, *"This Book of the Law shall not depart from your mouth, but you shall meditate in it day and night, that you may observe to do according to all that is written in it. For then you will make your way prosperous, and then you will have good success, "*indeed, you shall have good success when you hearken and observe to do according to all that is written in it! Please start doing so if you've not been giving your tithe. It may have been due to ignorance, but thank God that you've received knowledge! Be blessed and receive that *"outpour of the* *blessing with not enough room to contain"*as promised by God.

Chapter 4

The Free-will Offering

"Then the LORD spoke to Moses, saying: "Speak to the children of Israel, that they bring Me an offering. From everyone who gives it willingly with his heart you shall take My offering."
Exodus 25:1-2

The free-will offering is an offering given in the house of God for its upkeep and to undertake new projects. A typical free-will offering is seen in Exodus 25:1-8, where the children of Israel, in their sojourning through the wilderness from Egypt, had to bring an offering in order to build a tabernacle for God. God told Moses, who was their leader, to ask the people to bring an offering to the Lord to erect the Tabernacle for Him.

"Then the LORD spoke to Moses, saying: "Speak to the children of Israel, that they bring Me an offering. From everyone who gives it willingly with his heart, you shall take My offering. And this is the offering which you shall take from them: gold, silver, and bronze; blue, purple, and scarlet thread, fine linen, and goats' hair; ram skins dyed red, badger skins, and acacia wood; oil for the light, and spices for the anointing oil and for the sweet incense; onyx stones, and stones to be set in the ephod and in the breastplate. And let them make Me a sanctuary, that I may dwell among them."

A very important thing to note about this offering is that it must be given willingly from the heart. It is described as a "free will" offering. Yes, God is asking that it be given but not demanding it. You are not obliged to give nor do so under compulsion. God was very specific in telling Moses to take the offering "from everyone who gives it willingly with his heart." In other words, do not take an offering from anyone who is unwilling to do so from the heart. Wow, this is interesting! Is it possible that people have given a "so-called" offering to the Lord, but it was not acceptable in His sight? Could God have rejected people and their offerings? I believe so; therefore, let us be mindful of how we give our freewill offerings to God.

We are not obliged to do so; it should be given from a willing heart. Another thing to note is that God asked for the various things that were needed to build the sanctuary for Him. In the same vein, in our present day, we realize that there are some things that are needed in the house of God to maintain it, like paying utility bills including gas, electricity, water, cable, garbage, and the like. The sanctuary needs cleaning on a consistent basis as well as other maintenance services. So we ought to give our offering, bearing in mind that there are needs in the church. Sometimes, there are projects to be carried out like building a new sanctuary or building an addition. In such cases, it becomes obvious that we increase our offering because of the greater need beyond the norm. Some churches call it building or project funds, and special offerings are taken for such purposes. These offerings once again are to be given from a willing heart.

On addressing the free will offering, the Apostle Paul, in his letter to the Corinthians, devotes an entire chapter to it in 2 Corinthians 9. This signifies the absolute importance of the free-will offering. *"Now concerning the ministering to the saints, it is superfluous for me to write to you; for I know your willingness, about* which I boast of you to the Macedonians, that Achaia was ready a year ago; and your zeal has stirred up the majority. Yet I have sent the brethren, lest our boasting of you should be in vain in this respect, that, as I said, you may be ready; lest if some Macedonians come with me and find you unprepared, we (not to mention you!) should be ashamed of this confident boasting. Therefore I thought it necessary to exhort the brethren to go to you ahead of time, and prepare your generous gift beforehand, which you had previously promised, that it may be ready as a matter of generosity and not as a grudging obligation. But this I say: He who sows sparingly will also reap sparingly, and he who sows bountifully will also reap bountifully. So let each one give as he purposes in his heart, not grudgingly or of necessity; for God loves a cheerful giver. And God is able to make all grace abound toward you, that you, always having all sufficiency in all things, may have an abundance for every good work. As it is written: "He has dispersed abroad, He has given to the poor; His righteousness endures forever."Now may He who supplies seed to the sower, and bread for food, supply and multiply the seed you have sown and increase the fruits of your righteousness, while you are enriched in everything for all liberality, which causes thanksgiving *through us to God. For the administration of this service not only supplies the needs of the saints, but also is abounding through many thanksgivings to God, while, through the proof of this ministry, they glorify God for the obedience of your confession to the gospel of Christ, and for your liberal sharing with them and all men, and by their prayer for you, who long for you because of the exceeding grace of God in you. Thanks be to God for His indescribable gift!"*

The church in Corinth was one that gave generously and willingly. There was this grace of God that was upon them to do so; thus, the Apostle Paul boasted of them to the other churches. Here, he exhorts them to continue in that grace so that his boasting of them will be justified when the other churches witnessed it for themselves. Once again, of significant note is their willingness to give "for I know your willingness" and their generosity "prepare your generous gift." These attributes of the free-will offering cannot be overemphasized. I believe this is what this entire chapter was devoted to by the Apostle Paul, and he brings those elements into play.

Just as God deemed the free-will offering to be given from the heart when He spoke to Moses to ask of the children of Israel, so it is with this exhortation as clearly noted in the verse 7: "So let each one give as he purposes in his heart, not grudgingly or of necessity; for God loves a cheerful giver." It is more about the condition of the heart with which one gives, but not necessarily the size of what one gives. It must never be felt or thought of as an obligation, and it shouldn't be given grudgingly. In essence, we must be cheerful and delighted to do so. This is God's requirement, which makes the offering acceptable to Him.

In terms of the generosity aspect, this is what the Apostle Paul had to say: "He who sows sparingly will also reap sparingly, and he who sows bountifully will also reap bountifully" Using the principle of sowing and reaping, he makes us understand that just as you reap what you sow, the measure of your giving will determine its outcome. If you sow little, you will reap little, and if you sow much, you will reap much. This principle is also expatiated by Jesus Himself in Luke 6:38: "Give, and it will be given to you: good measure, pressed down, shaken together, and running over will be put into your bosom. For with the same measure that you use, it will be measured back to you."

Jesus was also teaching on giving, which clearly indicates the free-will offering. Here, he encourages us to give bountifully because our giving is not in vain. Our giving is rewarded, and the measure of what we give is proportionate to which we shall receive back. Thus, the more we give, the more we receive. In this chapter, still on 2 Corinthians 9, the insurmountable benefits of the free-will offering are outlined. First, God is able to make all grace abound toward you, that you will always have all sufficiency in all things and may have an abundance for every good work. Second, as our giving goes to take care of the needs of the church and others like the poor, He causes our righteousness to endure forever. Third, God, who supplies seed to the sower and bread for food, will supply and multiply the seed you have sown and increase the fruits of your righteousness. Fourth, you will be enriched in everything for all liberality and cause many thanksgivings to God. Fifth, through the proof of this ministry of free-will offering, God will be glorified for the obedience of your confession to the gospel of Christ. Sixth, for your liberal sharing, you will be prayed for by those who long for you because of the exceeding grace of God in you. Wow! This is what becomes the divine or spiritual aspect of our free-will offering, which aligns with God's will. Sometime back, God gave me an insight into the divineness of our free-will offering, and I called it "The Eternal Memorial of Glory."

Eternal Memorial of Glory!

I believe this is a heavy-duty statement! Let us begin with the definitions of the keywords in this phrase. The definition of eternal is 'lasting or existing forever; without beginning or ending.' The definition of memorial is something established to remind people of a person or event. The definition of glory is from the Hebrew word 'Kabod,' which originally means 'weight or heaviness' but can also mean importance, honor, and majesty. Thus, putting all three words together, this statement in terms of the free will offering simply means to give an important or honorable offering that establishes one forever.

One of the few people who come to mind concerning this kind of offering is King David. He purposed in his heart to build a sanctuary for the Lord, and because of that, God established his throne forever, as seen in 2 Samuel 7:1-17 *"Now it came to pass when the king was dwelling in his house, and the LORD had given him rest from all his enemies all around, that the king said to Nathan the prophet, "See now, I dwell in a house of cedar, but the ark of God dwells inside tent curtains." Then Nathan said to the king, "Go, do all that is in your heart, for the LORD is with you." But it happened* that night that the word of the LORD came to Nathan, saying, "Go and tell My servant David, 'Thus says the LORD: "Would you build a house for Me to dwell in? For I have not dwelt in a house since the time that I brought the children of Israel up from Egypt, even to this day, but have moved about in a tent and in a tabernacle. Wherever I have moved about with all the children of Israel, have I ever spoken a word to anyone from the tribes of Israel, whom I commanded to shepherd My people Israel, saying, 'Why have you not built Me a house of cedar?' " ' Now therefore, thus shall you say to My servant David, 'Thus says the LORD of hosts: "I took you from the sheepfold, from following the sheep, to be ruler over My people, over Israel. And I have been with you wherever you have gone, and have cut off all your enemies from before you, and have made you a great name, like the name of the great men who are on the earth. Moreover I will appoint a place for My people Israel, and will plant them, that they may dwell in a place of their own and move no more; nor shall the sons of wickedness oppress them anymore, as previously, since the time that I commanded judges to be over My people Israel, and have caused you to rest from all your enemies. Also the LORD tells you that He will make you a house. "When your days are fulfilled and you rest with *your fathers, I will set up your seed after you, who will come from your body, and I will establish his kingdom. He shall build a house for My name, and I will establish the throne of his kingdom forever. I will be his Father, and he shall be My son. If he commits iniquity, I will chasten him with the rod of men and with the blows of the sons of men. But My mercy shall not depart from him, as I took it from Saul, whom I removed from before you. And your house and your kingdom shall be established forever before you. Your throne shall be established forever." According to all these words and according to all this vision, so Nathan spoke to David.*

This is one of my favorite scripture readings. David had in his heart to build a house for God. What an amazing man! He loved God so much that the thought of him living in a cedar house while the Ark of the Lord dwelt in tent curtains did not seem right to him. He thought God deserved far better. Here we can see the elements of the free will offering come into play.

It was an offering that firstly emanated from his heart. When he spoke to Nathan about his plans, "Then Nathan said to the king, *"Go, do all that is in your heart, for the LORD is with you."* King David was not obliged to do so. God did not ask him to do so as he talks about it to Nathan the prophet - "have I ever spoken a word to anyone from the tribes of Israel, whom I commanded to shepherd My people Israel, saying, 'Why have you not built Me a house of cedar?' Thus we can see that this thought of David greatly pleased the Lord because it was not a command from Him; rather, it was the thought of David's heart. After those statements, God proceeded to pronounce blessings on David and on his house forever.

There is an irony that occurs in this scripture. Instead of David building the house for God, God chose David's son to do so and not only that, but God now tells David that He (God) will build him (David) a house- "Also the LORD tells you that He will make you a house." Just the thought of his heart got him a house from God and an unprecedented blessing. One thing I've come to know in my walk with God is that you can never out-give God. Whatever you give to God, He turns it into a blessing that is beyond measure for you. Yes, this is the God we serve, and He is patiently waiting for your seed to multiply it and turn them into fruits.

The magnitude of the blessing God pronounced on David is mind-boggling. Firstly, God was going to fully establish the nation of Israel by giving them a place and also rest from all their enemies. Secondly, after David's death, his son, the fruit of his body, will ascend the throne. God will be with him, and this son will build a house for the Lord. My favorite part of the blessing is that even when his children sin, he will punish them but will not take away His mercies from them. This is what is referred to as the "sure mercies of David," an everlasting covenant with God. God promised that even though his seed may depart from Him, He will always restore them and bring them back unto Himself. Thank God for the gift of Jesus Christ, who is also the natural seed of David, through whom we have all become partakers of this everlasting covenant.

God also gave David the blessing of perpetual kingship in Judah – *"And your house and your kingdom shall be established forever before you. Your throne shall be established forever."* Once again, thank God that through this natural lineage and by His divine orchestration, we have also become kings and priests as seen in Revelations 1:6 "And hath made us kings and priests unto God and his Father; to him be glory and dominion forever and ever. Amen" and in 1Peter 2:9, *"But ye are a chosen generation, a royal priesthood, a holy nation, a peculiar people; that ye should show forth the praises of him who hath called you out of darkness into his marvelous light."* What a blessing obtained through a free-will offering! Characteristic of the free-will offering is generosity. Even though God asked him not to build the house for Him, he made provision of what will be needed for it. David gave very generously towards the House of the Lord as seen in 1 Chronicles 29:1-5: *"Furthermore King David said to all the assembly: "My son Solomon, whom alone God has chosen, is young and inexperienced; and the work is great because the temple is not for man but for the LORD God. Now for the house of my God, I have prepared with all my might: gold for things to be made of gold, silver for things of silver, bronze for things of bronze, iron for things of iron, wood for things of wood, onyx stones, stones to be set, glistening stones of various colors, all kinds of precious stones, and marble slabs in abundance. Moreover, because I have set my affection on the house of my God, I have given to the house of my God, over and above all that I have prepared for the holy house, my own special treasure of gold and silver: three thousand talents of gold, of the gold of Ophir, and seven thousandtalents of refined silver, to overlay the walls of the houses; the gold for things of gold and the silver for things of silver, and for all kinds of work to be done by the hands of craftsmen. Who then is willing to consecrate himself this day to the LORD?"*

Anytime a free-will offering is given, it is done with much generosity. King David gave so much gold, silver, bronze, iron, wood, and different kinds of stones. He says because of his love for God and having set his heart on the house of God, he gave over and above all that he had prepared. It is therefore not surprising how God blessed him beyond measure, once again, confirming Jesus' words in Luke 6:38: *"Give, and it will be given to you: good measure, pressed down, shaken together, and running over will be put into your bosom. For with the same measure that you use, it will be measured back to you."*

Another free-will offering with an eternal memorial of glory is that of Mary of Bethany. She is always referred to as the woman with the Alabaster Jar of Perfume. She gave it as an offering from her heart, and, beyond that, it was more than a generous offering. In Matthew 26:6-13, *" And when Jesus was in Bethany at the house of Simon the leper, a woman came to Him having an alabaster flask of very costly fragrant oil, and she poured it on His head as He sat at the table. But when His disciples saw it, they were indignant, saying, "Why this waste? For this fragrant oil might have been sold for much and given*

71

to the poor."But when Jesus was aware of it, He said to them, "Why do you trouble the woman? For she has done a good work for Me. For you have the poor with you always, but Me you do not have always. For in pouring this fragrant oil on My body, she did it for My burial. Assuredly, I say to you, wherever this gospel is preached in the whole world, what this woman has done will also be told as a memorial to her."

Mary of Bethany came to the place where Jesus was and poured oil on His head. No one had asked her to do so, but I believe she did it from her heart. Unbeknownst to her, she met a need that Jesus did not request for, just like David deciding to build a house for God without being asked to do so. It was a need because Jesus said, "she has done a good work for Me... For in pouring this fragrant oil on My body, she did it for My burial." This is the more reason why we should freely give unto God beyond our first fruits and tithes. You never know what your offering will accomplish in the kingdom of God. It will surely meet a need of God. I'm sure someone is wondering, "how can God have needs?" We are God's children and physical representatives of Him. Thus to meet our needs, which become His needs, He has to use human instruments to satisfy them. When we give freely to the church, people come to the knowledge of Jesus through the programs offered by the church, and their lives are impacted forever. This is a great need of God that is satisfied through us.

Again, Mary of Bethany's offering was so generous to the extent that some of the disciples became angry because of its cost. The oil she poured on Jesus is described as "very costly fragrant oil." In some bible versions of this story, it says that it was the equivalent of a year's salary. Hence, the angry disciples thought it was a waste of money and that it could have been sold and given to the poor, but Jesus rebuked them. What Jesus' rebuke means is that God is deserving of our generous offerings. Once again, Mary of Bethany also received a timeless, immeasurable blessing from the Lord. Jesus said that "wherever this gospel is preached in the whole world, what this woman has done will also be told as a memorial to her" Can you imagine that? Well, here we are, writing and reading about her because of a free-will offering she gave unto the Lord. What about the man called Cornelius, whose giving came as a memorial before God? When we read from the scriptures in Acts 10, this was a man who feared God and generously gave alms to people. An angel of God visited him and told him that his prayers and alms had come up as a memorial before God. The story reads: "There was a certain man in Caesarea called Cornelius, a centurion of what was called the Italian Regiment, a devout man and one who feared God with all his household, who gave alms generously to the people and prayed to God always. About the ninth hour of the day, he saw clearly in a vision an angel of God coming in and saying to him, "Cornelius!"4 And when he observed him, he was afraid and said, "What is it, lord?" So he said to him, "Your prayers and your alms have come up for a memorial before God." He was asked by the angel of God to bring in Apostle Peter to his house and that he would tell him what to do. To summarize the entire story of Acts 10, at the end of this chapter, Cornelius and his entire household, including his relatives and close friends, received salvation, the baptism of the Holy Spirit, and were baptized in water. They were all ushered into eternal life, which is what the memorial of glory is all about. He gave willingly from his heart, and not only that but his giving was described as generous. We are told he gave alms, which we will look into details in the next chapter. Can God testify of your offering as a memorial? Be provoked unto good works by Cornelius' example.

The Shunnamite woman in 2 Kings 4 also gave generously to

the man of God, and in return, God blessed her with a son, for she had no child, and her husband was advanced in years. *"Now it happened one day that Elisha went to Shunem, where there was a notable woman, and she persuaded him to eat some food. So it was, as often as he passed by, he would turn in there to eat some food. And she said to her husband, "Look now, I know that this is a holy man of God, who passes by us regularly. Please, let us make a small upper room on the wall; and let us put a bed for him there, and a table and a chair and a lampstand; so it will be, whenever he comes to us, he can turn in there."*

Time and space will fail me to talk about Abraham, who, through faith and obedience, when he was tested by God, offered his only son Isaac to God. Through this act, God gave him an eternal blessing as seen in Genesis 22:16-18 ... *"By Myself I have sworn, says the LORD, because you have done this thing, and have not withheld your son, your only son— blessing I will bless you, and multiplying I will multiply your descendants as the stars of the heaven and as the sand which is on the seashore; and your descendants shall possess the gate of their enemies. In your seed all the nations of the earth shall be blessed, because you have obeyed My voice."* Every believer or person of faith's blessing is identified with Abraham. God promised him that in his Seed, who is The Christ, shall all the nations of the earth be blessed. What a memorial! This is about the ultimate with regards to the men who received memorials of glory.

To God be all the glory as He is the one who offered the utmost sacrifice or offering of His free will. The magnanimity of His heart and generosity is immeasurable and indescribable. By virtue of the offering of His only begotten Son, Jesus Christ on Calvary, the precious blood of God was shed, that you and I may have eternal life. As seen in Romans 11:17, we have become partakers of the olive tree, the root and fatness there off. Can you also have a memorial of glory? Yes, I believe each and every one of us can. I know that my life is a product of this kind of offering. My mother did something that has made me who I am today. I believe she gave an offering that pleased God, rendering it an offering of eternal value and a memorial of glory.

Personal Story on Eternal Memorial of Glory

As I mentioned earlier, I believe that I'm a product of this memorial of glory. I believe my children and children's children are going to be. They will continue to

76

eternity because it is an inheritance of eternal blessing.

Don't be jealous of me or begin to wonder what about you. Before I share my story, I want you to know you are a product of this memorial of eternal glory. I'm sure you may be wondering how. Well, the answer is very simple. As we read from the beginning that giving is a spiritual act that transcends the natural by God giving us His only begotten son and by the virtue of you accepting this precious gift of God, you become a partaker of His divine nature.

In 2 Peter1:2-3, scripture tells us that *"His divine power has given to us all things that pertain to life and godliness, through the knowledge of Him who called us by glory and virtue, by which have been given to us exceedingly great and precious promises, that through these you may be partakers of the divine nature, having escaped the corruption that is in the world through lust."* Now you are to continuously pursue this godliness, God's divine nature. In our pursuit of godliness (becoming like God) through prayer, fasting, giving, etc., even as you have accepted the gift of God, which is Jesus Christ, you have inherited the eternal blessing or memorial of glory through our Lord Jesus Christ.

77

Now let me continue with my story, knowing that you are no more jealous of me. Haha! When my mother became a born-again believer, she pursued God with all her heart in every way she could. She attended prayer meetings, bible studies, women's meetings, and, of course, was regular at Sunday worship services. She prayed very much on her own and studied the word of God.

I can remember always hearing her praying in tongues or praying in the spirit (a very funny language to me then). I remember her setting time aside for family bible devotion, though not on a regular basis. One of the things she did so well was in her giving, as I mentioned earlier, with regard to the paying of her tithes. I believe that when it came to her giving of free-will offering, she gave her best, and most importantly, it touched the heart of God.

Like David and the woman with the alabaster jar, she received the eternal blessing that will continue to run in the family. Through her, my dad, my siblings, and I came to the saving knowledge of Jesus and became born-again believers. All she did was continuously pray for us, invite us to church and continue in her pursuit of godliness. When

78

we happened to go to church with her, we were convicted of sin, righteousness, and judgment and gave our lives to Christ. We became connected to and adopted in the family of God, hence, triggering the eternal blessing through Christ Jesus.

On a very personal note and testimony, one of my siblings, even though he had accepted Jesus Christ as his Lord and Savior, was still very carnal. At a point it looked like he had lost true fellowship with Christ. However, just as God promised David in 2 Samuel 17:14-15 that *"I will be his Father, and he shall be My son. If he commits iniquity, I will chasten him with the rod of men and with the blows of the sons of men. But My mercy shall not depart from him."* Even though things were not going too well with this sibling of mine, at every turn in his life, it looked like an invisible hand or grace of God was upon him and delivered him from every difficult situation. One thing my mom had desired was for all her children to graduate from college. In his late years, this sibling of mine graduated from college, fulfilling my mom's dreams. He's now happily married with children and walking in the faith that was passed down to him. It is amazing how almost everything my mom prayed for and desired God to do in our lives, including our marriages, career, and health, have come into manifestation.

This is what God can and will do for us. Thank God for a mother who passed on an eternal blessing. She gave so much towards special projects in the church and the like, even with her little. You can also do so and should. After you have accepted Jesus Christ as your Lord and Savior, move beyond that and pursue godliness, and in the area of your giving, trigger that eternal blessing! Yes, you can, and God is waiting on you!

Chapter 5

Alms

"He who has pity on the poor lends to the LORD, And He will pay back what he has given.:"
Proverbs 19:17

Alms are things such as money, clothes, food, etc., given freely to relieve the poor. We usually distribute alms to the needy. Alms in our modern-day are sometimes referred to as charity. Charity also simply means generosity and helpfulness, especially toward the needy or the suffering; in other words, aid given to those in need. Also, an institution engaged in the relief of the poor is referred to as a Charity, and the public provision for the relief of the needy is also referred to as charity.

Unlike the firstfruits and tithes which God mandates, or even the freewill offering that we give of our own accord to God, the alms is a loan to God and scripture is very specific on that in Proverbs 19:17: *"He who has pity on the poor lends to the*

81

LORD, And He will pay back what he has given." If God sees our giving to the poor as loaning to Him, then this certainly is the heartthrob of God, and thus, the need to do so cannot be overemphasized. It also means that anytime we give to the poor or needy, we are standing in the stead of God or doing so for God. Remember, God is a spirit, and He requires human instruments to carry forth His work in the natural even though the work is of a spiritual significance. This is why the giving of alms is beyond a natural thing. It has a deep-rooted spiritual significance, as we'll get to know as we continue reading.

Do not miss out on an opportunity!

Having known what alms are and how God deems them worthy, what a privilege and honor it is to have the opportunity to serve in the stead of God and also get whatever you give back from God! In Matt 19:16-21, Jesus encounters the rich young ruler whom he gave the opportunity to give to the poor to receive eternal life and be perfected in God. *"Now behold, one came and said to Him, "Good Teacher, what good thing shall I do that I may have eternal life?" So He said to him, "Why do you call Me good? No one is good but*

One, that is, God. But if you want to enter into life, keep the commandments." He said to Him, "Which ones?"Jesus said, "'You shall not murder,' 'You shall not commit adultery,' 'You shall not steal,' 'You shall not bear false witness,' 'Honor your father and your mother,' and, 'You shall love your neighbor as yourself.' "The young man said to Him, "All these things I have kept from my youth. What do I still lack?"Jesus said to him, "If you want to be perfect, go, sell what you have and give to the poor, and you will have treasure in heaven; and come, follow Me. But when the young man heard that saying, he went away sorrowful, for he had great possessions."

Here Jesus counseled the rich young ruler to sell all he had and give the proceeds to the poor; for in doing so, he would be perfected. This young man came to Jesus inquiring how he may obtain eternal life, and Jesus told him to keep the commandments of which He elaborated on in the scripture. The young man explained to Jesus that he had kept all those commandments since he was young, but he still felt something was missing in life. He proceeded to ask Jesus what it was, and the surprising answer Jesus gave to him was to give alms. We are told he was very saddened by Jesus' answer because he had great possessions. Was he able to do what Jesus told him to do? I guess not because he did not rejoice that he had found the answer to the missing puzzle in his life.

He was to give away what he had to be perfected, and not only that but also to have treasures in heaven. Jesus also asked him to "come follow" Him after he heeded His admonition. Is materialism becoming a hindrance for some people from following Christ and becoming perfected in Him? I believe so. True love of the Father requires that we come to the realization of putting Him first in everything and all other things secondary because the truth is that, after we have put Him first, He will make provision for everything else we need or desire. The challenge is letting go of everything for Christ and that is what proves that we love Him. Unlike the rich young ruler, do not miss out on an opportunity!

Endeavor to take advantage of every opportunity to be a blessing to the poor and the needy because it is the Father's heart desire. Trust me, if you can do this, you can obey all the commandments because you would have been perfected!

God's Approved Fast

At a time when the children of Israel were complaining about God not accepting their fasting nor acknowledging them, God showed them the kind of fasting He approves of, and once again, it had to do with the giving of alms. In Isaiah 58:7-8 scripture says:

"Is it a fast that I have chosen, A day for a man to afflict his soul? Is it to bow down his head like a bulrush, And to spread out sackcloth and ashes? Would you call this a fast, And an acceptable day to the LORD? "Is this not the fast that I have chosen: To loose the bonds of wickedness, To undo the heavy burdens, To let the oppressed go free, And that you break every yoke? Is it not to share your bread with the hungry, And that you bring to your house the poor who are cast out; When you see the naked, that you cover him, And not hide yourself from your own flesh? Then your light shall break forth like the morning, Your healing shall spring forth speedily, And your righteousness shall go before you; The glory of the LORD shall be your rear guard"

Here, God tells us of the deep spiritual significance of fasting beyond the mere outward portrayal. Fasting is not just the abstinence from food, the show of humility by bowing down the head or spreading sackcloth and sitting in ashes. Rather, it is dealing away with oppression, wickedness, and bondages. God admonishes them that what pleases Him is feeding the poor, clothing the naked, and providing shelter to the homeless, and as always, the Lord comes in with His reward, which in this case is breaking forth from obscurity into light, receiving healing and being adjudged righteous. We cannot out-give God when it comes to alms. He will surely pay you back. It may not be the exact thing you gave out but in a different area where you have a need, as in the case above. They were to seek God by meeting God's needs, and God, in turn, would pay them back with the blessing they need.

Alms and Eternal Judgment

What has the giving of alms got to do with judgment? Almsgiving has got everything to do with eternal judgment, and not only that but virtually with everything we do and live for, because when all is said and done, when we exit the earthly portals of life, it will be a determinant of where we spend eternity. In Matthew 25:31-46, scripture says:

"When the Son of Man comes in His glory, and all the holy angels with Him, then He will sit on the throne of His glory. All the nations will be gathered before Him, and He will separate them one from another, as a shepherd divides his sheep from the goats. And He will set the sheep on His right hand, but the goats on the left. Then the King will say to those on His right hand, 'Come, you blessed of My Father, inherit the kingdom prepared for you from the foundation of the world: for I was hungry and you gave Me food; I was thirsty and you gave Me drink; I was a stranger and you took Me in; I was naked and you clothed Me; I was sick and you visited Me; I was in prison and you came to Me.'

"Then the righteous will answer Him, saying, 'Lord, when did we see You hungry and feed You, or thirsty and give You drink? When did we see You a stranger and take You in, or naked and clothe You? Or when did we see You sick, or in prison, and come to You?' And the King will answer and say to them, 'Assuredly, I say to you, inasmuch as you did it to one of the least of these My brethren, you did it to Me.'
"Then He will also say to those on the left hand, 'Depart from Me, you cursed, into the everlasting fire prepared for the devil and his angels: for I was hungry and you gave Me no food; I was

thirsty and you gave Me no drink; I was a stranger and you did not take Me in, naked and you did not clothe Me, sick and in prison and you did not visit Me.'"Then they also will answer Him, saying, 'Lord, when did we see You hungry or thirsty or a stranger or naked or sick or in prison, and did not minister to You, Then He will answer them, saying, 'Assuredly, I say to you, inasmuch as you did not do it to one of the least of these, you did not do it to Me.' And these will go away into everlasting punishment, but the righteous into eternal life."

Wow! Can you believe what you are reading in this scripture? Yes, you must because that is coming from Jesus Christ Himself. Simply put, Jesus is saying that your works towards the poor, needy, less privileged, and the like will be judged. If you are found not to have responded in a favorable manner, you'll suffer damnation; but if you helped, then you will inherit the kingdom of God. God identifies with the poor and needy; thus, whatever you do to them, you are inevitably doing it to Him.

God does not only identify with the poor and needy, but He also has a responsibility towards them; therefore, when you give to them, not only have you given to God, but you have given for Him. In other words, you have given in God's stead, and that is why God promises to pay you back. In the above scripture, we realize that it is payback time, and both the righteous and unrighteous are surprised. Thank God for this parable of Christ as an admonition to prepare us for what lies ahead of us.

Beyond this parable, in the book of Revelations, where Jesus reveals Himself to His beloved Apostle John, on the Island of Patmos through visions, Revelations 20:11-12 says that *"Then I saw a great white throne and Him who sat on it, from whose face the earth and the heaven fled away. And there was found no place for them. And I saw the dead, small and great, standing before God, and books were opened. And another book was opened, which is the Book of Life. And the dead were judged according to their works, by the things which were written in the books."*

God judged the dead according to their works written in their books. This emphasizes the truth that our works go beyond this temporal earth we live in and that after we die, judgment awaits us whether we met God's standards or fell short of His expectations. Scripture is established by two or three witnesses. Let us be mindful of our giving in all areas, and especially not to forget or take for granted the giving of alms, for we will be judged on it.

True Neighbor

Who is a neighbor? The definition of neighbor is simply someone living or located near another or fellow man. However, Jesus has changed this narrative. Jesus' definition of neighbor is found in the Good Samaritan parable found in Luke 10:25-37.

And behold, a certain lawyer stood up and tested Him, saying, "Teacher, what shall I do to inherit eternal life?" He said to him, "What is written in the law? What is your reading of it?"7 So he answered and said, "'You shall love the LORD your God with all your heart, with all your soul, with all your strength, and with all your mind,' and 'your neighbor as yourself.'" And He said to him, "You have answered rightly; do this and you will live." But he, wanting to justify himself, said to Jesus, "And who is my neighbor?" Then Jesus answered and said: "A certain man went down from Jerusalem to Jericho, and fell among thieves, who stripped him of his clothing, wounded him, and departed, leaving him half dead. Now by chance a certain priest came down that road. And when he saw him, he passed by on the other side. Likewise a Levite, when he arrived at the place, came and looked, and passed by on the other side. But a certain Samaritan, as he journeyed, came where he was. And when he saw him, he had compassion. So he went to him and bandaged his wounds, pouring on oil and wine; and he set him on his own animal, brought him to an inn, and took care of him. On the next day, when he departed, he took out two denarii, gave them to the innkeeper, and said to him, 'Take care of him; and whatever more you spend, when I come again, I will repay you.' So which of these three do you think was neighbor to him who fell among the thieves?" And he said, "He who showed mercy on him." Then Jesus said to him, "Go and do likewise."

In this parable, just like that of the rich young ruler, a lawyer wanting to test Jesus asked Him a very poignant question about how one might inherit eternal life. As was Jesus' manner, He responded with a question of which the lawyer answered rightly and that was, ' *"You shall love the LORD your God with all your heart, with all your soul, with all your strength, and with all your mind,' and 'your neighbor as yourself."* The discourse did not end there. The lawyer further asked Jesus who his neighbor was. This led to Jesus redefining neighbor beyond anything we have known. In summary, from the above scripture, a

91

man on the verge of death had three men come his way, but only one of them, a Samaritan, came to his aid. Interestingly enough, the other two who did not help him were a Priest and a Levite. Jesus asked the lawyer who among the three was a neighbor, and obviously, it was the Samaritan who showed mercy to the dying man. Jesus told him, "Go and do likewise." Once again, Jesus has portrayed a very beautiful image that captures what it means to give alms. We can see and understand clearly from this parable that it is giving help to the helpless, providing for the needy, poor, and weak and the like. It is simply sharing your fortune with the less fortunate. In so doing, as we have been admonished earlier, we are giving to God and giving in God's stead and He will pay us back. Will you qualify as far as God's definition of who a neighbor is? The Priest and the Levite failed to qualify. They were too busy in carrying out their own agenda that they forgot about what truly mattered in the sight of God. This is what happens with most us. We tend to focus on routines and rituals, turning the worship of God into a religion instead of having a relationship and fellowship with Him, getting to know His heartbeat and carrying it out. In our pursuit of religion, God is taken out of the equation. We end up with a strange product that is not a byproduct of God as we are presently witnessing among so-called Christians. Just as

Jesus admonished the lawyer to "go and do likewise," may we also do likewise and become the neighbor God desires us to be.

Let us return to God and His simple principle of almsgiving. In 1 John 3:16-17, scripture beautifully summarizes what the love of God is and what we ought to do to show that we also abide in God and show forth His love. *"By this, we know love, because He laid down His life for us. And we also ought to lay down our lives for the brethren. But whoever has this world's goods, and sees his brother in need, and shuts up his heart from him, how does the love of God abide in him?"* God's love is shown to us by the giving of Himself to us, and this is what we have to do for others to show that the love of God is in us. We must demonstrate the love of God by responding to the needs of others; other than that, nothing shows that the love of the father is in us. It is as simple as that. Remember that all our works will follow us into eternity, by which we will be judged. Revelations 14:13 says, *"Then I heard a voice from heaven saying to me, "Write: 'Blessed are the dead who die in the Lord from now on." "Yes," says the Spirit, "that they may rest from their labors, and their works follow them."*

What is your testimony at this time, or is it still in process? A very dear friend of mine shared hers with me when I made her aware that I was in the process of writing this book. In her own words, Mrs. Gertrude Kumi wrote, "I remember back in Ghana at my workplace, the cleaner approached me to ask for a small loan. At that moment, the money I had on me was almost equal to what she asked, but I gave it to her and told her that there was no need to refund it. The following day I received that amount with an additional, "0", Glory to God." Wow, isn't it an amazing testimony? She gave, and she received right back, confirming God's word that He will pay us back when we give to the poor and needy. I also have similar testimonies where I had been a blessing to someone and quickly had a greater blessing in return. Among many of them was a time when I decided to be a blessing to a family by cooking for them now and then. On one of the days, while I was packing food for this family, it struck me that my 22-year-old son, Isaac Jr., was living in Indianapolis all by himself. He had just finished college and was working in that city. As any doting mom will, I wondered how he was eating and coping. As I was packaging the food, I whispered to myself, "I wish I could cook some of this food for my son." I really was thinking about him the whole time. So in the course of the week, I called to check upon him. I asked him what he was eating and how his cooking skills were coming along. You won't believe what he told me. He said, "Mom, this week, my fridge is packed with so much food." He said, "There is this Deaconess in the church I've been attending who has been so pleased with my faithfulness and commitment to God. She says I'm her adopted son, and she cooked so much food for me this week—from Jollof rice to soups and Fufu, etc. She has a son of my age and a daughter with special needs just like us, so she sees me as part of her family and has promised to make sure that she occasionally brings me home-cooked food when she comes to church." I was dumbfounded. What a God we serve! Look at the exceedingly unexpected blessing of God. He did what I couldn't do for my son, even as I was doing it for another family. Indeed, we serve a true and a living God. He pays us back indeed!

Chapter 6
Honor God!

"Honor the LORD with your possessions, And with the firstfruits of all your increase; So your barns will be filled with plenty, And your vats will overflow with new wine."
Proverbs 3:9-10

To honor someone is to highly esteem them and regard them with great respect. In so doing, we appreciate, recognize, and admire them. Not only that, but we also become thoughtful, attentive, and considerate of their wishes, feelings, and rights. I believe that as children of God, honoring God should become our number one priority. Everything we live for and do should revolve around this truth.

God desires and expects us to honor Him as our Father, which is rightly so. After all, He created us for His pleasure as seen in Isaiah 43:21 *"This people I have formed for Myself; They shall declare My praise,"* and Revelations 4: 11 says *"Thou art worthy, O Lord, to receive glory and honor and power: for thou hast created all things, and for thy pleasure they are and were created."* However, like in all things, including His commandments, God gives us our will to choose. He does not force His will on us. Nonetheless, we must always face and live with the consequences of our choices and decisions.

In His commandments from the beginning in Exodus 20:12, we are admonished to honor our parents, which has a great reward of well-being and long life. *"Honor your father and your mother, that your days may be long upon the land which the LORD your God is giving you"* The Apostle Paul reiterates this commandment also in Ephesians 6:1-3 *"Children, obey your parents in the Lord, for this is right. "Honor your father and mother," which is the first commandment with promise: "that it may be well with you and you may live long on the earth."* If God, the creator and author of all things, including mankind, who knows the end of a thing from the beginning, commands us to honor our parents, then we better be up to that task. Not only that, but among the Ten Commandments given, this is the only commandment that comes with a promise. Thus, the commandment to honor one's parents is very great indeed. However, I am also inclined to believe that the reverse may apply in the sense that if you do not honor your parents, it will not be well with you and your days on earth will be cut short. It is as simple as that. Let us stick with the positive end of this bargain, and hopefully, we will not dare to venture into the negative side of this commandment.

Parents have a great responsibility towards their children, which never ends even when they become adults. As a parent, I can identify with this responsibility from conception through childbirth and babyhood. Not to mention the difficult toddler age (the terrible twos and threes), childhood, teenage, and young adult years. I remember one day telling my mom that now that all her children have become adults, she doesn't have a care in the world and should be enjoying life. She said it was not so. Using me as an example, she said that despite being grown and accomplished as a married woman with children, she still has a sense of responsibility towards me. She has to pray daily for me and my siblings, her grandchildren, in-laws, and the like, that all will continue to be well with us. More so, as a Christian, we will all be Christians and walk in the knowledge and fear of God. At this stage of my life, I've come to greatly appreciate what my mom said back then. Having a teenager and three young adult children, I realize that the work and responsibility of the parent never ends. It only takes a different turn at the different stages of life. Therefore is it a big thing that God is commanding us to honor our parents? Absolutely not! Just as they have a responsibility towards us at all times, we are obliged to honor them as well.

If the commandment to honor our parents brings well-being and long life which is about everything one can desire, then it will be intriguing to know the reward of honoring the Almighty God. If there is anything like that, can you imagine it? Yes, I strongly believe there is, and if we actually honor God, the rewards are definitely going to be mind-boggling. Just as our parents have a responsibility towards us and we are obliged to honor them, God is not just our heavenly Father, He is our creator, author, and sustainer of our life, and as such, we have an even greater obligation to honor Him. Just as I said from the beginning, this should be our number one priority and all that we should live for, because once again, the rewards are indescribable.

God's Desire for Honor

God has a strong desire for us to honor Him. God's desire for us to honor Him is shown in Malachi 1:6-8 – *"A son honors his father, and a servant his master. If then I am the Father, Where is My honor? And if I am a Master, Where is My reverence? Says the Lord of hosts to you priests who despise My name. Yet you say, 'In what way have we despised Your* name?' "You offer defiled food on My altar but say, 'In what way have we defiled You?' By saying, 'The table of the Lord is contemptible.' And when you offer the blind as a sacrifice, Is it not evil? And when you offer the lame and sick, is it not evil? Offer it then to your governor! Would he be pleased with you? Would he accept you favorably?" Says the Lord of hosts." In the days of the prophet Malachi, the priests and the people cared less about God, and clearly, God was very grieved with them. As a Father, He wants His children to honor Him, and as a Master, He wants His servants to give Him reverence. Is this a hard thing to ask of His people? Their actions had clearly shown that they lightly esteemed God. These actions were seen in the kind of offerings they gave unto God. In our relationship with God, our offering speaks volumes of how much we love and appreciate God. Based on how much each person has, it may not be necessarily the quantity but the quality. We are obliged to give our best to God. As we can see from the above scripture, they gave defiled food, blind, lame, and sick animals as offerings to God. These are things that they would not dare give to their earthly leaders. If they do this to God, it is clearly a sign of utter disrespect. In spite of this grave sin on their part, they still had the audacity to ask God what they had done wrong. Clearly, as God has pointed out, their wrong is spelled out in their giving. Our giving matters to God, but most importantly, He is interested in the quality of what we give.

Honoring God should not be mere lip service but the condition of one's heart. In Isaiah 29:13, scripture says, *"Therefore the Lord said: "Inasmuch as these people draw near with their mouths and honor Me with their lips but have removed their hearts far from Me, and their fear toward Me is taught by the commandment of men."* It is very sad to note that God is grieved with the people for their lack of respect for Him as their God. So it is with this generation. Many proclaim love for God, but it is merely lip service. Clearly, our honor for God should be seen through our actions. The professed fear for God has become a mundane religious activity. Religion is a manmade tradition, whereas the true love for God and a relationship with Him emanates from one's heart. One does not need to be told to do something before it is done; otherwise, it has become a religion or tradition of men. May our hearts return to the father of all spirits. This yearning of God for our honor is mentioned in the dispensation of the second person of the Trinity. Jesus reiterates this in Matthew 15:7-*"Hypocrites! Well did Isaiah prophesy about you, saying: 'These people draw near to Me* with their mouth, And honor Me with their lips, but their heart is far from Me." Affirming what was spoken by the prophet Isaiah, Jesus notes how men honor God with their lips but not from their hearts. If Jesus reiterated this statement, then the importance of honoring God from the heart cannot be overemphasized. Again, Jesus stated in John 5:23 that *"That all may honor the Son, just as they honor the Father. Whoever does not honor the Son does not honor the Father who sent him."* Here, not only are we to honor the Father, but we are to honor the Son, Jesus Christ. They are three persons in one God, God the Father, God the Son, and God the Holy Spirit. This, in essence, means that we are to honor the Holy Spirit as well. That is why in our present time, in the dispensation of the Holy Spirit, the Apostle Peter under His inspiration wrote in 1 Peter 3:15: *"But in your hearts honor Christ the Lord as holy, always being prepared to make a defense to anyone who asks you for a reason for the hope that is in you; yet do it with gentleness and respect."* We need to give honor to the Trinity beyond mere words but from our hearts just as Peter puts, *"But in your hearts honor Christ the Lord"* God is asking that we honor Him, likewise is Jesus and Peter under the inspiration of the Holy Spirit. I never saw it so stark in my life until now. We must therefore seriously heed to this call. Now the question is, how do we honor God beyond lip service but from the heart? God has a modus operandi in place for us and this is what my husband calls, "God's Prescribed Honor."

God's Prescribed Honor

Scriptures clearly show us how to honor God. Among the many portions of scripture to this effect includes one that communicates this truth clearly in Proverbs 3:9-10 – *"Honor the LORD with your possessions, And with the firstfruits of all your increase; So your barns will be filled with plenty, And your vats will overflow with new wine."* Here, the scripture does not mince words on exactly what must be done to honor God and that is to give Him *"the firstfruits of all your increase."* We are not to give Him "some" but "all" of our increase. This is where it becomes challenging for some people but the truth is that you cannot serve God partially. My husband always says that the best definition of a word is that same word. Thus, when scripture says all, it means all. This is where we sometimes get things wrong by trying to redefine God's standard, and worst of all is when we try to silence the voice of our conscience by saying or assuming that God understands when we know we are not doing the right thing. In doing so, we try to reduce God to our standard, which is dishonoring Him right there. He alone is God, and His word is above all else, and we must deem it so, tremble at it, hearken to it, and obey it, thus bringing honor to Him. This is why in Malachi 1:6-8, God was specific about how He has been dishonored, and that is His name being despised by the people offering defiled food at the Lord's table. It wasn't the best they could give to God. *"You offer defiled food on My altar ... you offer the blind as a sacrifice, Is it not evil? ... you offer the lame and sick, is it not evil? Offer it then to your governor! Would he be pleased with you? Would he accept you favorably?" Says the Lord of hosts,"* Let us take God at His word and do as He requires of us without tweaking it to suit our whims and caprices. Once again, all means all and not some. Scripture says, *"Honor the LORD with your possessions, And with the firstfruits of all your increase."* Now another question is, are we truly giving to God the "firsts" or anything we deem okay, or even our "lasts" or "leftovers?" God is not our dog to be given leftovers, He is not even our equal to give Him whatever we deem okay, but He is our Master, Creator, and Father and must be given what He chooses to receive. We should even desire to go over and above what He's asking of us if we can afford it for our offering to be acceptable in His sight. As simple as it looks and sounds, let us remember the stark difference between Cain and Abel's offering, even as one led to curses while the other became *"a more excellent sacrifice."* Abel gave of the "firstlings of his flock," and not only that, but scripture says *"and their fat thereof."* Let us give to God what He deserves and desires, and He will bless us without measure.

Also, in order to honor God, it must not be just lip service but from the heart. It is not surprising that God said the people honor me with their lips, but their hearts are far from me. Jesus also quoted this same scripture. The question now is, "how do we honor God from the heart?" Well, Jesus gave a clear answer to that in Matthew 6:21: *"For where your treasure is, there your heart will be also."* Once again, it comes down to your treasure. My son always says that God is such a great business partner, and he will sign up with Him again and again as his business partner. If we acknowledge that God is the one who has created us, given us breath and strength to go about our lives, and given us the power to get wealth, then what is the big deal in honoring Him with our treasure by giving our firstfruits, tithes, freewill offering and alms? If God is asking that you give Him the firsts of your harvest, the tenth of your increase, any freewill offering out of your heart and have mercy on the poor out of all that you have, and all that is left is yours, then what a great deal it is! Assuming God, as a shrewd business partner, did not only ask for the firstfruits but also the "secondfruits" in addition, or say because He created you and gave you the power to get wealth, He demands 51% of your increase as tithes, or actually gave you a percentage in regards to your offering and alms, how would we feel? We realize clearly that it is not necessarily about the substance given, but the condition of your heart towards God, how much you love Him and are ready to obey Him beyond and above what He requires of you. That is what it means when Jesus said, "For where your treasure is, there your heart will be also." God makes it clear in scriptures that if we honor Him, He will honor us as well as seen in 1Samuel 2:30b, ... for those who honor Me I will honor, and those who despise Me will be lightly esteemed." This is not rocket science; it is the plain truth which must be well understood by everyone. As we do unto the Father, so He shall do unto us through others. You reap what you sow; you don't sow apples and reap bananas. As we honor the Lord, all His promises of blessings that come with it shall be ours, but if we don't, then all the curses of not doing

106

so shall become our portion. What is your choice? As a matter of fact, we all desire to be honored even as our Father desires, so let's make the right choice to honor God so that we would also be honored by Him. If for no other reason, just for the love of God for us, let us honor Him as our love for Him, for He is far beyond any treasure here on earth that we can have.

Chapter 7

The Conclusion
"The earth is the Lord's and the fullness thereof; the world and they that dwell therein."
Psalm 24:1

I trust that you have been inspired and enlightened in the preceding chapters of this book. Now the question is, "what is next?" We have heard this saying that knowledge is power. The wise king Solomon in Proverbs 18:15 says, *"An intelligent heart acquires knowledge, and the ear of the wise seeks knowledge."* What have we learned so far? Have we gained any insight at all? Have we added on to our existing knowledge and understanding? It is my prayer that your answer will be an emphatic "Yes!"

Wrapping up everything that has been said, first, let's remember that it is God who created the heavens and the earth and all that is in it just as the scripture clearly tells us in Psalm 24:1: *"The earth is the Lords and the fullness thereof; the world and they that dwell therein."* He created Adam- Mankind, put breath in him, placed him in the garden to till it and he became accountable to God. So is our life: we are not of our own. He has made us, and we are accountable to Him. We cannot choose to live outside this truth as some people choose to. The truth is that, whether we choose to do so or not, in the final analysis, we will face our creator for judgment as scripture declares in Hebrews 9:27 that "... it is appointed for men to die once, but after this the judgment."

When it comes down to earthly wealth and goods, we are simply stewards and custodians. All that we have has been given to us by God, both Melchizedek and Abraham referred to God at the time when he tithed as El-Elyon, the possessor of the heavens and the earth in Genesis 14:19-22 *"Blessed be Abram of God Most High, Possessor of heaven and earth; And blessed be God Most High, Who has delivered your enemies into your hand."* And he gave him a tithe of all. Now the king of Sodom said to Abram, *"Give me the persons, and take the goods for yourself."* But Abram said to the king of Sodom, "I have raised my hand to the LORD, God Most High, the Possessor of heaven and earth" Indeed, God is the owner of everything. If we have that clear understanding, we will not have any problem in giving back to Him what is due Him. Sometimes, there is the deception of thinking that we worked hard for whatever we have or acquired by our own strength. In Deuteronomy 8:18a, scripture says, *"And you shall remember the Lord your God, for it is He who gives you power to get wealth."* It is God who gives us the ability and strength to get whatever we have. Without God, we can do nothing.

What do we do with this wealth and all that He has given to us and made us custodians of? Well, God has given clear and specific directions on what to do, and we have to do so. We do not have any excuses at this point. The word of God in Acts 17:30 says, "And the times of this ignorance God winked at; but now commands all men everywhere to repent." Moreover, ignorance is no excuse, and the consequences are the same.

Firstly, as we have read from the preceding chapters, we are to give our firstfruits unto God. We are to do so through the church that He has set us in. God clearly made it known in the time of Cain and Abel that He demands it! When Cain failed to do so, God told him that if he had done well, he would have been accepted, and the sin that was crouching at his door wouldn't have taken hold of him. Why am I repeating this scripture? It is for our benefit even as in several portions of the word of God, the Apostle Paul says, that for me to be redundant is for your benefit. I believe this is to the benefit of some of us. Some people have chosen to turn a blind eye with regards to giving their firstfruits which is very scary. Once again, God clearly states that all the "firsts of the firsts" belong to Him in Exodus 13:2. He says, *"Consecrate to Me all the firstborn, whatever opens the womb among the children of Israel, both of man and beast; it is Mine."* Let's remember the spiritual significance and benefits, as was reiterated by the Apostle Paul in Hebrews 11:4 with regards to Abel's offering. *"By faith Abel offered to God a more excellent sacrifice than Cain, through which he obtained witness that he was righteous, God testifying of his gifts; and through it he being dead still speaks."* If God gave to us His first and only begotten son, making us all a kind of firstfruits unto Himself, then we are to honor His word and give Him our firstfruits.

Secondly, we are to give our tithes to the Lord through his chosen ministers. Remember, the tithes are given to the Priests and the Levites because that is their inheritance in God. They did not receive any inheritance; thus, everything offered to God, in terms of the tithes and firstfruits, goes to them. Apostle Paul reiterates this in 1 Corinthians 9:13-14: "Do you not know that those who minister the holy things eat of the things of the temple, and those who serve at the altar partake of the offerings of the altar? Even so, the Lord has commanded that those who preach the gospel should live from the gospel." However, we must bear in mind that though here on earth our tithes are received of men, as scripture says in Hebrews 7:8, "Here mortal men receive tithes, but there he receives them, of whom it is witnessed that he lives," our offerings are received by the one who lives forever, God, beyond the natural realm.

Surprisingly, many people regard the giving of firstfruits and tithes as an Old Testament principle or that which was of the law, and as such don't care to adhere to it. Just as a reminder and a caution, I want to emphasize that these principles of giving the firstfruits and tithes were done before the law came into existence, as witnessed through Abel, Abraham, and Jacob. It was incorporated into the law of Moses, and in the time of the Judges and prophets, they were adhered to. In the time of Jesus, in the dispensation of God the Son and the dispensation of the Holy Spirit, they were clearly practiced. After all, Jesus said He came to establish the law, not to abolish it, so the argument of the firstfruits and tithing being obsolete is no more a reason not to give, and this argument is nullified. Let us stay away from these excuses and allow the word of God and the Holy Spirit to direct us. As I always say, I'd rather obey God in error than disobey Him in ignorance.

People's failures to give their tithes have had dire consequences in their lives and that of the church, and it continues to do so in our present times. Many fine men and women of God have had to quit doing the work of God because financially, they can't be supported and have had to pursue secular jobs. Many of them are also bi-vocational. A few actually love it, but most of them do so in order to be financially stable to support their families.

This causes the church of God to suffer because God's work is not carried out fully as it is supposed to be. That is why God says that "ye have robbed me" when we refuse to pay our tithes and offerings. The storehouse of the Lord is empty in many churches. It is rather unfortunate because many people compare the average church with the mega-churches out there. Those mega-churches, whose pastors have private jets and live in mansions, etc., are about only 1% of all churches. The average pastor is unable to support themselves. Let us stop the comparison and do what God wants us to do to help the average church and its ministers. The ministers who have skewed this principle of God to the wrong direction only for their benefit and are abusing the people of God financially must stop doing so because God's judgment awaits them. May the average minister not suffer want but have more than enough to fully do the work of God through the giving of our tithes and firstfruits, causing God's name to be glorified and magnified.

When it comes to our freewill offering, I want us to remember David's offering and God's eternal blessing on his life. Remember all the personal testimonies shared. It will happen to you too if indeed you haven't experienced it. Break your alabaster jar like Mary of Bethany, and let there be an eternal memorial of glory on your stead. God sees and knows all that we do. Disobedience in giving freewill-offering also has dire consequences. It has been experienced in time past and our present days. Many churches in these present days are facing foreclosures. In my little lifetime, I have seen and heard of many churches being sold or foreclosed, and the sad thing is that, they are either turned into mosques or for secular uses, especially in Europe and America. How so sad! If every child of God and, for that matter, Christians will be faithful in their giving, we'll see the work of God move forward. As we have heard, again and again, the gospel is free but not cheap. We need money to build and sustain our churches. Projects in the church, including efforts at evangelism and outreach programs, need to be supported. I've been working in ministry for so long, and I know what I'm talking about – setting up our children's and youth ministries, building projects and management, etc. All these endeavors need continuous upkeep. Let us be a blessing to the church of God and let God's work continue.

Finally, with regards to almsgiving, which I believe is God's heartbeat, – I actually see God Himself in this picture as He said, *"whatever you do for these...you do unto me."* He also goes on to say that I will repay you because it is a loan unto me. Nobody in the world will suffer another day if we put this godly principle of almsgiving into practice. We have the poor and the needy all around us. Where are our bowels of compassion and mercy? How can you see your brother naked and not clothe him? Hunger must and can be eradicated if we all join in to support the weak and poor in our communities.

The surprising thing about everything I've written and said comes down to this – I am awed at God. I'm sure you'll be wondering why; the greatest revelation I received from this writing is this, that first, God demands that we give our firstfruits offering because it is His. There are no questions to be asked, no explanations needed. We just have to do so because it is His. When it comes to the tithes, He says we should pay it in order to have meat in His storehouse so that His priests would be taken care of. Here, I realize that if we don't do it, He calls us thieves and robbers, and it comes with the consequences of the devourer devouring us. When it comes to the freewill offering, He doesn't demand it, but if we do so, His blessing rests on us perpetually. There are no direct consequences if we don't give our freewill offering; however, we'll miss out on a permanent blessing. When it comes to alms, neither is it a freewill offering nor a compulsory demand, but it is a loan to God, which He promises to pay back. But guess what? That which our God didn't demand, request, or even ask us to give of our free will is what will determine our place in eternity! Think about it. As the elderly will say, a word to the wise is enough.

about it. As the elderly will say, a word to the wise is enough.

All I can say at this point is that fear God! Do His will and obey His principle in the area of firstfruits, tithes, offering, alms, and whatever special offering the Lord prompts you to give. He is a faithful God. He will bless you exceedingly. I am a testament to it. He will bless you to the thousand generations and beyond. I would err in obeying God than to disobey Him in ignorance.

Prayer / Confession

Dear Holy Spirit,

I thank you for the enlightenment and inspiration that you have shown and given to me through the pages of this book. I surrender my will, plan, and purpose for giving to you, and I fully embrace your plan and purpose for giving. Help me by your power that is at work in me to will and to obey your principle of giving. As I fully adhere to all these principles, I declare in the name of Jesus, in accordance with your word, that as I give my firstfruits, like Abel – you shall always testify of my offering as *"a more excellent sacrifice."* As I pay my tithes, as your word declares in Malachi 3:10-12, you will open for me the windows of heaven and pour out for me such blessing that there will not be room enough to receive it, and you will rebuke the devourer for my sake, so that he will not destroy the fruit of my ground, nor shall the vine fail to bear fruit for me in the field, and all nations will call me blessed, for I will be a delightful land. As I give my freewill offering - just as you blessed David and Mary of Bethany, I require such blessing upon my life and that of my children and children's children, an eternal memorial of glory, written in my heavenly books. And finally, as I give my alms, - you shall say to me as a righteous man or woman that I shall dwell and rule with you in eternity. Thank you, Lord, for your amazing gift of the principle of giving as it comes alive in my life. Thank you in Jesus' Name.

Amen.